Wonderful Letters to a Therapist

Library of Congress Catalog Number: 82-72815

ISBN 0-9609462-0-9

Printed in the United States of America

Wonderful Letters to a Therapist

Lou R. Owensby, M.S.W.
with Faison Covington

Foreword by
Ann Seagrave

Meridian Press

This book is dedicated to all those whose letters have been a part of reaching out to others who may be suffering as they once did.

CONTENTS

Wonderful Letters to a Therapist

Lou R. Owensby, M.S.W., A.C.S.W., is Director of Clinical Services at CHAANGE, the Center for Help for Agoraphobia/Anxiety through New Growth Experiences. Ms. Owensby was born in Jacksonville, Florida and received her B.S. degree from the University of Tampa, after which she began her graduate training at Tulane University School of Social Work and later at the University of Kansas School of Social Work, obtaining her Masters degree from the University of North Carolina (Chapel Hill) School of Social Work in 1967. Ms. Owensby has been a practicing psychotherapist for over fifteen years and has extensive experience in dealing effectively with agoraphobia and severe anxiety. Her experience includes medical and psychiatric social work. She was Assistant Professor at Queens College for five years before co-founding CHAANGE. Ms. Owensby is certified by the Academy of Certified Social Workers, and is a licensed Clinical Social Worker. She is a member of the American Orthopsychiatric Association and of the National Association of Social Workers. Ms. Owensby is married, has four children, and still maintains a limited private practice with her husband, Norman, who is a psychiatrist, certified by the American Board of Psychiatry and Neurology, and who serves as medical/psychiatric consultant to CHAANGE. The pioneering work of Lou Owensby and CHAANGE has been the subject of commentary by many television and radio programs as well as such national media as The Washington Post, Harper's Bazaar, The Los Angeles Times, Business Week, and Better Homes and Gardens.

Note from the Author -

As you read this book, you might want to ask yourself the following questions:

Do you often avoid doing things you wish you could do?

Do you find yourself making excuses because of your fears?

Does the feeling of not being in control frighten you?

Do you feel panicky for no apparent reason?

If you answered **yes** to any of these questions, you could have agoraphobia, the most severe anxiety a person can have. It is not just a fear of open spaces, and most agoraphobic men and women are not house-bound.

Agoraphobia limits different people in different ways. Some experience a feeling of discomfort in certain places, such as in church, in an automobile, in a super-market or in airplanes. Some have symptoms like dizziness, weakness, increased heart rate, nausea, sweating, confusion or a feeling of unreality.

Although you may not have to deal with this most severe anxiety yourself, you will find many ideas and suggestions which will help you know how to live a more satisfying and productive life.

If you do have agoraphobia, you will recognize yourself and find encouragement as well as specific help.

If you know someone who suffers with agoraphobia, you will better understand their "living hell." And, you will be better able to teach your children a healthy response to anxiety.

FOREWORD

In January, 1976, I experienced my first panic attack, and from that moment on my life changed dramatically and rapidly. It took but a few short weeks for uncontrollable fear to make a "believer" out of me and to turn my whole world upside down. I changed from independent to dependent, from gregarious to withdrawn, from extroverted to totally involved with inward recrimination, and worst of all, I changed from good old "steady-in-the-saddle" me, to OUT OF CONTROL.

Unless you have suffered with soul-shaking, pervasive fear, day in and day out, I am sure it would be hard to imagine how a seemingly intelligent person could be held prisoner by her own body and mind. But that is exactly what happened to me for over three years. I believed I was going insane by inches. I believed there was no help for me. I believed that no one else in the universe could possibly feel as terrified as I was feeling.

When I explained my feelings to my doctor, I got tranquilizers. When I explained my feelings to my psychologist, I got two years of philosophy. What I didn't get, was better.

In September, 1978, I began to get better the very moment that I met Lou Owensby. She assured me that I was neither crazy nor alone, gave me a name for my problem - agoraphobia - and started me on a four month process of changing how I thought, felt and behaved. I worked harder than I ever had in my life, but I was reinforced by my own desire to be rid of this paralyzing condition. I learned to live, to enjoy, to appreciate me. I was rewarded with a freedom that I had never imagined.

While I was busily working with my new skills, Faison Covington was going through the same process. Lou introduced us and tolerated hours of our comparing notes and raucous elation about how wonderful we were. Faison and I <u>did</u> feel wonderful, and after weeks of congratulating ourselves and each other, we convinced Lou that we were committed to sharing our feelings and to helping others in the same way that we had been helped.

In July, 1979, Lou, Faison and I organized CHAANGE, and since then we have had the privilege of working with thousands of agoraphobics. We feel close to each and every person who works with this process, and elated at every success. The letters we receive are filled with the same enthusiasm that Faison and I felt when we mastered new skills, and that enthusiasm means so much to all of us.

I know that I would not have felt so trapped by agoraphobia had I been aware of others who were experiencing the same feelings. I could have learned from them and taken hope from their victories. The pages of this book are filled with the very personal letters of those who had the determination to find a name for their misery, and the willingness to change life-long habits in order to reach their goals. Often, they will sing praises to CHAANGE, but please remember, as we do, that the credit belongs to the letter writer.

- Ann Seagrave

AGORAPHOBIA —
A
PERSONAL
HISTORY

The first letter I have chosen for this book is really more than a letter - it is a personal history and was written by a successful businesswoman who participated in the tape program, completing it recently.

Her transformation, as you will see from her story, has been and continues to be remarkable. I decided to begin this book with her story because it gives such a complete picture of the process of developing agoraphobia and of getting over it. Also, it sets the tone in an appropriate way, letting you, the reader, feel the hope, the determination, the work, the occasional agony and the pride involved in her struggle to change her patterns and habits which had led her to develop such intense and incapacitating anxiety.

Typical middle class family, that was mine. There was a father, mother, two children and a pet. My very early childhood memories are filled with visits to grandparents, aunts and uncles and my best friend. My sister was four years older and obviously thought I was in the way. I can remember how annoyed she would be to have to take me with her.

My father was a very mild mannered but quietly strong man. He was always the one I talked with. I believe he put forth every effort to be a good father to us. He was more able to talk about emotions and feelings but led a very disciplined life. He left most of the rule-making to my mother. He stood behind her on our discipline but yet I felt at times he disagreed.

My mother was a "neatnic." Everything had to be perfect. I assure you, you could have eaten off her floor. I realize now that she had a "should" list for herself that never ended. She also had a "can't" list that was quite long also. "You can't go to the movies or play cards on Sunday! ... You should go to church everytime the doors open. ... You must be a good girl because God is watching you. ... You must be a good girl and do as you are told so your life will be happy. ... If you do good things for other people, you will be happy. ... You must fear and love God or you'll go to hell." I am happy to say that she is a totally different personality today. However, I believe mine was a perfect background for agoraphobia. Somehow I came out of this feeling that if my performance was good other people would make me happy and would love me.

All of this was compounded by the fact that I was very jealous of my sister (this is a joke for us today because all the time she envied me – we are very close now). I felt I could never do anything that would make my parents and relatives as happy as my sister's lovely voice could do. Believe me, I spent a lot of time trying. I wanted to do enough to make everyone proud so they would make me happy and then I wouldn't feel so guilty that I couldn't sing for them. Never did I dream I was responsible for my own happiness. I cleaned, cooked, studied, went to church and tried to follow all the rules so these wonderful things would happen. I stopped expressing all of my own desires because I thought they may seem worthless.

Isn't it par for the course that when I married my first husband I carried almost all of the rules and shoulds with me? I tried to be the perfect wife, housekeeper and daughter-in-law. Yes, you could have eaten off my floor, too – probably off my driveway. I could handle anything. I got the job done. I was most capable. I should have realized that this was not the answer when this marriage ended in divorce.

COULD HANDLE ANYTHING

My two children were the center of my world. I tried to do everything to make their life perfect and happy. Somehow, they came out on top. They both have strong personalities and make their own decisions, right or wrong, and live their own life. I am most thankful to say they are also two of my very best friends. I never realized the stress that

3

I let build up when I was trying so hard to do for them.

During the years when my children were little, I started in the career I am in now. I worked very hard to be able to take care of us financially and to prove to myself I could be the best. Well, I went to the top, made a lot of money, but still was convinced that approval is performance-related and that I must strive to do even better, to be a better person and that would mean someone would make me happy. By this time I had remarried. You see, I thought I was right because he _did_ love me and make me happy; so all my efforts had been worth it.

With this marriage came four lovely stepchildren with a lot of emotional scars. Yes, again I thought I could be the perfect stepmother. It was almost as if I felt that if I could take on their problems for them, they would be just fine and, of course, I could handle anything. I failed to mention that four months after I remarried, two of my stepchildren came to live with me, and then several years later, a third came. What a circus. My husband and I were trying to adjust to marriage; my children were adjusting to a stepfather and a new place to live, and then here are two more with their own sets of problems who also have to adjust to a stepmother. Over those years I did feel the stress, but I still thought I could handle it. My husband left a career he had been in for 22 years to start another one, which was fine with me, but this left the total financial burden on my shoulders. All of this and a growing career never left any time for me, but of course, I didn't think I needed time for me. My body tried to say that it was too much, but I was deaf. After all, I had never learned to listen to it. The headaches started, then stomach problems. I developed food allergies. I was constantly tired, felt uneasy, confused and least of all happy. I tried counseling, tranquilizers, you name it. I was very upset with myself that I wasn't able to control it all. I beat myself up constantly.

I won the top award my company gives, something I truly wanted (good stress). My daughter was married (good stress), and I had a hysterectomy three days after the wedding. Superwoman!! I thought I went through all of this with flying colors. My main worry at this time was that my husband and I were starting to have problems. Now remember, I thought if I did all the right things, someone would be able to make me happy. I could come up with more things that my husband could do to make me happy. Lose weight - he did. Go to church with me - he did. Be what I want - he tried. What an impossible task. All the time I did not know that my happiness was in me, and that I had the right to make decisions and changes to bring about this happiness. I just became more critical of myself and everyone around me and started to withdraw.

FELT JITTERY

I noticed about four months after my surgery, that someone could come into my office to talk with me and I would get very jittery. If they stayed long enough, I would get very dizzy and feel as if I were going to faint. My secretary said I would turn chalk white. I thought that perhaps I had come back to work too soon (I stayed out 3 weeks) and this was just part of the recovery itself.

Then I noticed that in the morning when I was getting dressed, I would have the same feeling. I would get dressed, sit down and try to calm myself down until I could leave. Sometimes, I would be shaking so hard that I could hardly get out of the car when I got to work. My dialogue was, "What's wrong with you. You've got to get it together. WHAT IF you have a dizzy spell on top of this?"

Restaurants got to be impossible for me. I would get so nervous and dizzy, I would totally panic. I couldn't pick up the silverware or a glass. My neck would be so stiff it ached. I started totally avoiding restaurants.

The grocery store was just as bad. I would get halfway down one aisle and panic. I had to get out.

5

I would be almost nauseated when I got outside.

The panic grew in the mornings. On most days, I would force myself to get in the car, but then I couldn't drive. I would go back in the house, change into my jeans and spend the day worrying about what was wrong. The days I did get to work were pure hell. One panic attack after another. Then I started attacks of tachycardia. I wore an EKG monitor for 24 hrs. If you can believe it, I even hoped maybe that was the problem. After all, my father had died from a heart attack, so there was a chance I had something wrong. Well, I have a heart as healthy as can be. My doctor said all of this was stress-related and gave me a medicine to take to keep the beat regular. Well, believe me, it did not help one bit with the panic attacks.

This condition only grew worse. I would never go out to restaurants. I accepted no invitations to go out. I would come up with every excuse for someone to go to the grocery store with me or, better yet, go for me. I couldn't go to visit one of my best friends who is also a neighbor without having to leave. 90% of the time I could not drive to work. The few days that I made it, I would catch a ride and shake all the way in, only to start with the panicky feelings as soon as I opened my office door.

NEVER TOLD ANYONE

During all this time, I never truly told anyone exactly what was going on. My family knew I didn't feel well and was more withdrawn, but I couldn't tell them about the panic. They would truly think I was a nut. One of my stepdaughters had been through CHAANGE, and hinted that maybe this was what I needed. I completely refused to accept that as a possibility. Now I know that she could see through my facade. She left me a note saying that she loved me and if I ever needed her to please call her. She planted a seed.

The Christmas holidays came with stress on top of stress. We have a large family, and it takes a lot of work to get ready and, of course, all must be perfect. We had two new puppies, and my daughter and son-in-law were home with their dog. My mother and sister were also here. I was extremely panicky and nervous during these days. I felt as if I would totally jump out of my skin. I was better if I could stay in my house, but when we would go out it was awful. A couple of days after Christmas, I went to my room to take a shower. I started crying and could not stop. I was worried about my "condition." I was tired and the marital problems didn't get any better. My daughter took me to the doctor, who admitted me to the hospital for rest and some tests. All the tests were fine. I was put on Tranxene and sent home. My doctor said I was under too much stress and that I should relax and take my medicine. That was funny to me because I did not know how to relax.

Well, I was a good girl and did as I was told, but the medicine was not the answer at all. When I tried to go out of the house the same panicky feelings would hit me like a ton of bricks. I stopped taking the medicine then unless I was so bad that I could hardly stand it. Then the worst happened. I started to have panic attacks if anyone came to my house. I no longer had a safe place. I could have an attack just thinking someone might come. That did it for me. I remembered the things my stepdaughter had said, and thought I would try anything to get over this. It took me an hour to call her because I had a full blown panic attack thinking about it, and couldn't dial the number. When I did call, it took every effort to tell her what was happening to me and to ask if she thought I had agoraphobia. She gave me the number for CHAANGE, and assured me that I could get better. That's when I called. I waited until that night, and then I sat down with my husband and told him what I was going through. His response was one of shock that I had kept all this to myself.

...Little did I dream that not only was there help but a whole new life for me. I felt like a child at Christmas. Someone understood how terrifying the panic attacks were...

I was determined that I would follow the program to the letter and then surely I would get well very quickly. It was quite obvious to me that medicine was not the answer and I put all my faith into the program.

My stepdaughter came to see us for the weekend. She told my husband about the support and understanding I would need and how he could help me the most. This certainly was a big help. I believe the letter to family members I received is very helpful, but having someone who had gone through agoraphobia and CHAANGE talk directly with him and me made it so much easier. He believed what she said and did exactly what he needed to do to help me.

SURPRISED

I was surprised that when I first started listening to the relaxation tape I could feel the difference in my body. I was too quick to believe I could make it work but soon learned that you must, absolutely must, listen and work with the tape until it becomes a natural reaction and action for you. I had two copies. I listened in my car on the way to and from work. I listened at work and each night when I went to bed I listened again, doing the exercises. I found I was able to drive to work and do pretty well at work as long as I had my tape. It became my security blanket. In the first 7 or 8 weeks I must have played my tape fifty times a day. The people in my office and my family soon learned that when they saw the ear plug go in not to disturb me.

I was at the post office when it opened every Wednesday morning to get my weekly tape. Faison's remark about saying "I am calm and relaxed" <u>until you are</u> helped me so much. By repeating this statement to myself and using everything I had learned from my tapes I was able to go to a concert and restaurant. I was very tired after doing this but now I understood that I only had so much energy to use and I had used a tremendous amount going. I had finally learned to listen when my body said "I'm tired."

I also realized that I was no longer having headaches. This again was through listening to my body and doing for myself what I needed.

Well, lo and behold, I started to do things I had avoided ... only to realize after it was done that I wasn't frightened. I came home from the grocery store the first time and was putting up the groceries when I thought, "My Lord, it never entered my mind that I might have a panic attack." I just cried I was so happy. Other things didn't come so easily. The first time I went in a restaurant alone to meet a friend for lunch I worked on my relaxation until I thought I was alright. Sure enough about the time I had ordered my food here comes an attack. Well, I sat very still, mentally saying to myself that I was calm and relaxed, that I was having this attack because I had anticipated it because I had had them in restaurants before. My test was to see if I could pick up the glass of water in front of me. I kept saying float with it, don't fight it. I slowly reached for the glass, and I did it. I congratulated myself over and over for completing this small test so well and the attack left me. That was the beginning of the end of my fear of restaurants.

Statements that helped me a lot to get it together were that "people really do not spend that much time thinking about you" and that "when someone says something that hurts you, they are not saying it to you but for them." These two helped me end the constant trying to be perfect, worrying about what people thought and to not be so sensitive to what others said. In this I became able to allow myself to be less than perfect and then it all started to come together for me.

I was like Ann in that it became enough to fluff up the pillows and straighten up. I didn't have to clean myself into a tizzy. I could leave my bed unmade and do what I wanted to do. I finally learned how to be good to me rather than spending all my time and energy on others or trying to prove anything to anyone.

FROM ONE HECK OF A HOMEMAKER
TO ONE HECK OF A PERSON

The reaction from my family and friends was great. The more I let up on myself, the more they offered to help. I realized that there was very little I wanted to change about my husband. A lot of what I had fought to change were in reality his defenses. I could now understand his need for them. We have been able to communicate enough to work out our problem areas and are closer than we ever dreamed possible. I should add here that he listened to all of my tapes at least once and feels that he learned a great deal also. He kids me now that I used to be one heck of a homemaker but now I am one heck of a person. My friends ask me what has happened. They say I have a glow about me now. My boss says it would almost be worth having agoraphobia if everyone could end up as happy as I am. He only says that in innocence because he doesn't know what havoc agoraphobia can play with your life. I do believe there is a large part of the program which would help anyone.

I now do anything I CHOOSE to do. I have friends in for dinner and we go out a lot also. I'm traveling again in my work and love it. I make a point to have some time in each day for myself. I have learned to like myself and to respect my right to be what I am. I know that I don't have to be a good girl so somebody will love me and make me happy. I am a neat person and I make my own self happy. The happiness that other people bring into my life is icing on the cake. I have control of my life for the first time and I could never wish for more for anyone.

BACKGROUND

REQUESTS FOR HELP

Over the past months, we have received many letters which we knew would be supportive, insightful, and helpful for those who are suffering from that terribly limiting condition, agoraphobia. We knew we wanted to use them somehow - to help others - but we did not know how. Until we could decide, we continued to place these special letters in a large blue folder which was labeled "Wonderful Letter File." It recently became clear that the reason we had saved this correspondence was to write this book. It is our wish that these letters will give you information, inspiration, and hope in your own quest for a better life.

The letters that follow are typical of those received at CHAANGE, (The Center for Help for Agoraphobia/Anxiety through New Growth Experiences, Charlotte, N.C.), written by men and women of all ages, and from all walks of life, who have had to deal with agoraphobia, a most devastating condition. I have deliberately changed names, places, and situations to protect the identity of the 'letter writers'; however, except for that identifying information, the letters are exactly as they were written.

LEARNED BEHAVIOR

Traditionally, agoraphobia has been defined as a fear of open spaces, but recently has become known more accurately as a learned condition in which a person develops avoidance behaviors, usually multiple, because of an underlying or basic fear of becoming out of control, going crazy, painfully embarrassing themselves, and/or having a stroke or heart attack, or dying. Agoraphobia is at the same time the most severe anxiety as well as the most complex phobia; a condition which often has been missed, misunderstood, misdiagnosed and mistreated.

Before sharing the thoughts and lives of others with you, perhaps it would be good to give a little history of the organization, CHAANGE, which will help you understand the unusual circumstances in which these "wonderful letters" were sent.

THE CENTER

The Center was founded in May, 1979 in Charlotte, North Carolina. As a psychotherapist, I had been working for several months on an individual basis with two women who were suffering with agoraphobia. As each recovered, they expressed an interest in working with me to help educate others and to offer an effective treatment for those who also had this condition. Both had been in treatment before, unsuccessfully. One of the women, Faison Covington, had suffered for thirteen years, while Ann Seagrave had suffered for four years. The Charlotte Observer, the local newspaper, became interested and published a feature article about them and our work.

In response to requests for help generated by that newspaper article, the three of us began conducting structured groups in July of 1979, putting into practice the methods of treatment based on my understanding of the personality and background components of those who develop agoraphobia. The focus was on understanding the special sensitivities of those with agoraphobia, along with knowledge of the important role of non-productive thoughts, dialogue, and coping skills, and the development of more productive behaviors. After a period of months, during which time we had worked with many time-limited groups, it became clear that our methods were extremely effective in treating this condition which, heretofore, had been considered by many to be "intractable."

The Charlotte Observer article was later picked up by the Knight-Ridder wire service, creating a response from hundreds of people who wanted and needed help. At that time, (late 1979), there were very few appropriate, helpful treatment programs available for people suffering with agoraphobia, and the Center received countless requests for help from all over the country. It was in response to the need of those who could not be away from home or business to go to an office for treatment, that the CHAANGE tape cassette program evolved. It is from participants in the tape program, who are from all over the world, that these "wonderful letters" have been received. For an idea of just how desperate those with agoraphobia often feel, listen to a young 22-year-old woman from the East, who had just received our free "introductory packet" which includes a tape explaining our program:

I just received your material on January 27, and I was so excited when I found the package in my mail box, I wanted to scream.

Shared the material and tapes with some of my friends and they were interested and supportive.

After I finished reading all the material you sent me, I wished there had been more. I wanted to cry, knowing there's help for me. I was very touched by the other people's experiences - it made me feel very close to them.

I thank God for your organization and people that know what to do for this condition and are willing to help everyone that suffers with it.

Thank you for everything and I will be waiting impatiently for the program to start.

PROGRESSION

And, this letter from another young lady, just beginning the program, will give you some understanding of the progression of this condition:

...I have had agoraphobia for under a year. I have only recently discovered (one week ago) that this is in fact what I have. It was through listening to the first tape that I made this remarkable discovery.

I, too, ran from doctor to doctor to try to find a cure for all of the horrible physical symptoms

14

I was experiencing. The dizziness, problematic breathing, sweaty palms, blurred vision, hot flushes, etc. really made me feel dreadful, and not getting any relief or answers was worse.

I, like most agoraphobics, can recall my first panic attack vividly. It was a Thursday night in March of 1980. I was driving home from work after having had dinner with some people from the office. It was dark, raining very hard, and my windshield wipers were not working well. About two miles from home, my body went berserk. I got home safely, but I was unable to tell my parents what had really happened (because I didn't know). I only told them I wasn't feeling well. The next day my fiance took me to the doctor. The doctor said that I was hyperventilating. He also said I was very tense. He attributed this to the following: A) I was getting married in five months or so - I had never lived away from home for any appreciable length of time and am very close to my family, and B) I was marrying a man who had a dangerous job. The doctor suggested I see a psychiatrist to work this all out. I did visit a therapist who was somewhat helpful. She told me I was experiencing "separation anxiety" and that I was pushing myself too hard. I visited her twice only. I was fortunate enough to be relieved of my symptoms for the next few months.

Planning our wedding was the important thing and, luckily, I felt great during this time. We were married and I must tell you it was a dream come true.

TERRIBLE PANIC

The day I returned to work after a two week honeymoon, I had a terrible panic attack during lunch. This is when I went back to the therapist, who helped but not like the first time around. Then I started going to all kinds of doctors - no answers.

I am now unable to go to the supermarket comfortably, driving to and from work is a problem, the hairdresser is out of the question completely, *attending social and business functions is not easy, although I do go when I absolutely must. I haven't been to church in over three months, which I miss terribly.*

Interesting enough, I do go to work everyday. Driving has become a little better since I've read your literature and listened to the tape. However, once I reach work I am very anxious throughout the day (for which there is no reason). I eat lunch alone, for which I make some excuse because I feel terribly uncomfortable otherwise.

Once I reach home at night, I am back to my old self again, unless I know I have to go out. In that case, I am anxious once again.

I realize that my agoraphobia is not as severe as some of the others, but I also know I can't go on like this.

Up to this point in my life, I have been most blessed. I have a wonderful husband and family, a good job (that I do well and also enjoy), a close circle of friends, good health, a college education, no financial problems, etc. Perhaps this is why it was difficult for me to understand how I developed agoraphobia, when it seemed I had so much going for me.

I realize now, knowing "the why" is not part of the getting well process.

I can't begin to tell you the tremendous feeling I had listening to the tape. 1. As I already mentioned, the discovery of what I have. 2. That I am not alone. 3. I am not having a breakdown. 4. Probably the most important thing – the light at the end of the tunnel, i.e. there is a cure and one which I am most confident will work. I eagerly await the arrival of my tapes so that I can begin my "re-learning process" at once.

And, from a 31 year old man:

I have had these anxiety problems for the last four or five years. It just kind of sneaked up on me. I went to doctors who said there was nothing physically wrong.

Thinking that I was going crazy, I went to a psychiatrist. He did help me. He tried to teach me to relax. It is easier said than done. Three years ago, I was off work for two straight months, virtually a prisoner in my house, afraid to go out. I have improved 1000%. Absenteeism is not a problem at work now, but every day is a battle. I work in Data Processing. In my job, I must regularly go to meetings and take training classes to keep up with the 'state of the art'. I feel trapped in meetings and classes. I don't ever feel comfortable taking my wife and young daughter out to dinner.

If your program helps me, I will be eternally grateful. I feel if I lick this problem, I can more efficiently perform my job, be a better husband and father, and lead a <u>much happier</u> life.

MISUNDERSTOOD

To give an example of how this condition is often misunderstood and misdiagnosed, here is a letter from a doctor who has just discovered himself that agoraphobia is what he suffers from:

...I am 76 years old and practiced as a G.P. for 50 years and was never smart enough to make a diagnosis of agoraphobia - although in looking over my records, I know I should have. No consultant I ever called came up with that diagnosis. In fact, I had to look up the spelling. None of my medical books even mentions it, and treatment is grouped with all other phobias under "phobic anxiety syndrome" and the treatment is "relieve the cause of anxiety", as you know....

THERAPEUTIC DIALOGUE

Included in the Tape Program are fifteen tapes which are sent weekly (plus a relaxation tape), and homework assignments, plus additional materials and books. The program is presented as a therapeutic dialogue. It is based on a combination of cognitive, behavioral, and goal-oriented theories and therapies, and is purposefully focused on the listener's needs to achieve an atmosphere similar to one that the listener would encounter if participating in person. Examples of our success in achieving that atmosphere follow.

A professional man in a 'middle America' state writes:

I know I have made great progress with the CHAANGE program because I don't feel guilty for being so late in writing this letter. Because of a long business trip, the holidays, and a two-week round of illness in our family I have required longer than 15 weeks to complete the program. I want to share some of my thoughts and feelings now that I have completed the course.

This past week has been a very good one for me in showing me that I have made great strides in my efforts to change some of my old habitual emotional responses to the world around me. I have not had a full panic attack since the beginning of the program. In fact, the last day I had an attack was the day the introductory material from you arrived in the mail. I was so tired of enduring the embarrassment and pain of living with my condition, I didn't know it had a name, that I knew I had to do something constructive and positive to gain control of myself. I hoped CHAANGE would help me do that, and I can say now it has and I have.

I was so relieved to find out what I had and why I had it. What a joy to realize for sure that I wasn't mentally ill or psychologically abnormal.

As I have listened to the tapes and done the homework and relaxation exercises, I have had a slowly growing feeling of confidence and positive energy. I have learned much about myself and been able to see myself and my life in a new way. I have come to realize that agoraphobia is not a cause, but an effect. It is only a symptom that something is out of balance or harmony. I have discovered why my life has unfolded as it has, and why - I in particular

- developed the specific symptom of agoraphobia.

I will not go into detail of all the little things that have happened this past several weeks. But I can tell you that now I have a strong belief that I am much better in control of my life now than I was four months ago. I will not say I am in complete control of my life because I do not think that is possible or even desirable. That is one thing I have learned - to begin to give up trying to control everything around me, including myself. When I try to control constantly, I shut myself off from the power and supply of the universe, which is trying to help me all the time. Trusting a power, greater and outside of myself, has helped me release my hold on myself.

LOOKING TO THE FUTURE

As I look to my future, I have a sense of great benefit from having suffered with agoraphobia this past twelve years. As you said on one of the tapes, "I can be much better and wiser and stronger because of my agoraphobia." But now, I am ready to transcend this part of my life and move on to bigger and better experiences.

I really want and need to tell you how grateful I am for your work and caring that has made my recovery possible. I would like to stay in touch with you for at least a while through the newsletter, so I can use your services as I continue to practice my lifestyle changes. I know there may be times ahead when I could use some of your resources to help me. I know I am on a journey that I will never complete, but that doesn't frighten me anymore. You have helped me realize that the journey is the destination. May God bless you Lou, and Ann, and Faison on your life journey.

A 39 year old woman from a university town in the East:

THANKS!! I have recently completed your fifteen week course on agoraphobia <u>and I feel so good!!</u>

It is difficult to capture my feelings in a letter, but I'll give it a try.

The background facts are pretty typical. My parents divorced when I was eight years old. My mother was an alcoholic, but coming from a prominent family, we tried to hide that fact. Our roles were reversed early and I feel that I missed most of the childhood years. I did continue to do all the "right" things - graduated from college, worked and continued to try to care for a critically ill mother for quite a few years, until her death. In the meantime, I had met and married a kind, compassionate fellow and will celebrate our 18th anniversary in a couple of months. Our first child was born only weeks after my mother's death. Within two years, just as we were beginning to get to know one another again, my father was killed in an automobile accident. Soon thereafter, came a move to a new city, a new practice for my husband, and a second child arrived. Such rapid changes are indeed difficult for one lacking in life skills.

I believe that learning the meaning of <u>compassion</u> was a major start for me. It seemed to be lacking (or temporarily lost) in my life. Treating myself kindly - and I didn't know that I wasn't - has made a great difference to me and how I now view and treat my family and friends. My body "thanks" me often now by feeling rested and relaxed instead of being plagued with all the old symptoms I had suffered with for years. As I have mentioned earlier, I had always managed to keep going and doing, but was constantly on guard - always anxious, wondering, worrying. <u>That is all changing now!</u> It has been great to become familiar with my initial signs of fatigue, stress and anxiety and be able to deal with them before they become overwhelming. I have also been able to stop <u>pushing</u> myself constantly and take time to "recover" physically or emotionally if the need arises. That has paid great dividends. Now I have day after day when I feel really great and have energy left over in the evening.

I have begun letting go of my strong tendency to control others - and not any too soon. My 15 year old and I are beginning to enjoy each other's company.

Even though I am still daily digesting all this new information, I feel <u>so</u> fortunate that I can now share these skills with our children.

You all have introduced flexibility to me. My husband just commented as I was writing this on how I have accepted and dealt with numerous frustrating events and situations. That is something I was not able to do at all before.

A BONUS

So much of what I have learned during these weeks are what I would call a bonus. Their benefits are subtle - almost indirect. At first, the facts seemed almost unrelated to my agoraphobia. However, as time passed, I see that as I absorb the information, there is a very tangible difference in my general attitude and approach to life. On closer examination, I am aware that it was, in part, the lack of this information that contributed to the possibility of developing agoraphobia.

These skills are not all mine yet and I accept that - I have plenty of time to practice. Distracting myself and dialoging to overcome negative, anticipatory thoughts continues to be hard, but, I do see progress. I am doing many <u>new</u> things and am also able to do most of the "old" things very comfortably -- without worry, without panic. It is wonderful!

You all should surely be proud of your work and the results. I am really encouraged to know that the public is becoming more aware of agoraphobia and hope that you continue your efforts in this area.

I shall enjoy replaying the tapes and re-reading all the literature for a long time. The newsletters are invaluable! Again, thank you for all the knowledge, strength and encouragement.

And, a 27 year old woman from another eastern state:

Here is my #15 lesson. I have not completed #14, but I have not forgotten it. So many times over the past fifteen weeks, I have written out my life story

21

to you, but then decided not to mail it, because after I was finished, it didn't seem necessary. I said what I needed to say and understood it better each time I wrote it.

You don't know what all of you mean to me at this point in my life. You all have been my life for the few weeks gone by. I am a very romantic person and when I read love stories, (or really, any book I read), I never want them to end - I want to just keep reading about the characters and find out what happens to them. Well, Ann, you, Lou, Faison and myself have been the characters in the story! I never want that friendship to end. As you have probably well guessed, there are tears of sadness and happiness.

I have made a promise to myself that if I ever get the chance, I will meet you. We always go through Charlotte on our way to the beach.

I have started my tapes all over again and hear something different each time - the same words - my ears are different now.

I will have to go now. I have several appointments this morning and I have no makeup left, but we will keep in touch.

CAN CHANGE MYSELF

and,

...I want to thank you for showing me that there is someone out there who understands our problem. I lived for thirteen years, going from one doctor to another, hearing the same thing, "It's just nerves. Take a pill, it will help!" But it didn't help.

Then my friends, even my family, started to wonder. My friends became fewer because I couldn't drive, couldn't sit through a meeting, or even attend a dance comfortably. My family started to say, "it's all in your head. You can do it if you really wanted to." No one really understood. Until you came along! I really appreciate you!

I know I have a long way to go yet, but I've also come a long way!

I have to share something with you. I have always felt that a lot of my problems stem from the treatment I had gotten from my parents, aunts, uncles, etc., although I knew it wasn't the full reason why I developed severe anxiety. I just couldn't pin things down. Last night I went to an aunt's house and could see how critical they really are of me and my children. It was an eye-opener! I do not blame anyone, but I can see how I felt around them. Now I can have a different reaction to them than I did before. It's how I react that counts! I can't change them, but I can change myself! My habits, my thinking. I have control over myself and my reactions. Thank God for you. I am coming along a lot better now. Maybe this year I may even drive in the snow, which is something I have feared for a long, long time. I must change my dialogue to myself. I will try, thanks to you.

THE CONTENT

The content of the fifteen week program is structured to encompass four general areas: 1) understanding the condition and why and how one happened to develop it, 2) learning relaxation skills so that one can use them automatically as a tool or technique for coping, 3) learning new and more productive ways of dialoguing to oneself and with others and, 4) using the new techniques, skills and tools as one begins to practice the things that have been avoided until he/she is in control of his/her life again. It is a fifteen week process, with each week building on the last. The focus is on helping the participant change the attitudes and negative patterns of thinking which have fed into the agoraphobic condition, as well as on the avoidance behavior itself. In this way, one develops the skill to make deliberate choices which will enable him/her to keep from ever getting into the agoraphobic spiral again. Each tape is presented as a therapeutic dialogue in which the therapist and recovered agoraphobic talk with each other, covering the concepts and principles involved in mastering the necessary skills to get over the condition of agoraphobia or severe anxiety. It explains exactly what one needs to do to get back in control of his/her life again, and encourages one to do it.

From the East again:

...I was a very "typical" agoraphobic with all the symptoms - very much like Ann and Faison. I, fortunately, read about you and your work in the Grit newspaper. My development of the condition was also typical - background, etc.
First, let me say that your approach to treating agoraphobia with stressing the relaxation tape is brilliant. It is truly imperative to relax in the beginning of treatment. That helped me enormously. The description and explanation of agoraphobia's development is also wonderful for me. It is absolutely necessary to know that there is a name for this condition and that others have it. I cannot stress the importance of knowing "what is wrong" enough. That, alone, freed me. The other concept that was so helpful was learning about habit. I never knew that anxiety, fear, panic could be part of habit. I now can say to myself, "this is only habit." What a relief to know this!! This idea takes the terror out of "nerves" and fear and anxiety and makes them just another bad habit.
The third major breakthrough for me was learning about finite energy. I truly needed to learn not to fear fatigue. I actually used to get afraid if I became tired at any time but night. I can see in hindsight that a lot of my problems started when I was overtired. However, my main panic attack came after I came down from the O.R. after a miscarriage. That panic started at the precise moment I began to wake up and continued - off and on - day or night - for two years. However, I had suffered more mildly from the condition prior to that. The miscarriage did magnify the latent problem. I am not listing my personal symp-

toms of panic, as I know you've heard them all many times, and there's no need to go over them for you.

Now, Lou, I can begin to tell you about my progress so far. My main and glorious news is that I no longer rely on Tranxene at all anymore. The use of tranquilizers was devastating for my ego. I just hated to take them, but I needed them for anxiety. I never took more than prescribed, but, even so, I knew I was too young to rely on them so strongly.

My next important breakthrough is that I am never afraid alone in the house. I don't scare myself at home, ever. I have stayed alone at night, (never could before), for three nights when my husband had to travel on business. Before CHAANGE, I always had friends stay over with me, and I didn't like that about myself. I was so proud when I was able to stay alone, and my friends kept calling to see if I was all right! Before CHAANGE, I hyperventilated so badly alone at night that I would begin to pass out. What got me through being afraid of being alone, day or night, were, 1. relaxation, 2. distraction. These two tools are indispensible to me now. The relaxation tape kept me from getting tense enough to hyperventilate, and the distraction kept me relaxed.

The third problem for me, driving alone, has been moderately successful. I can now drive much farther than I could. I must still keep pushing and practicing to drive far distances - this I know will come with diligence - so I'm not worried about it. But I'm excited to try the new driving tape!

Lou, I have merely highlighted my progress so far. I know how busy you are and hesitated to send you a book!! Suffice it to say, I am happy again!! I like me - agoraphobia and all!! I'm a lot less afraid and dialogue positively a lot.

I feel I know you so well and I'm close to you, Faison and Ann. Ann is totally responsible for my "getting into" the program as she has allowed me to pay monthly, and wrote to me about it. For that kindness, I shall always be in Ann's debt. I thank Faison for being so honest and giving, and allowing me to find myself in her many times! Both Ann and Faison

25

are the greatest and I love them for what they shared with me. That leaves you, dear Lou. What can I say to you? You have taught me more than any psychologist did in three years! I relax the moment I hear your voice on the tape. You gave me hope, knowledge, approval, the ability to find humor in my personality, and the strength to change. You are truly blessed with knowledge and the ability to help others with your knowledge. I hope I can meet you one day.

DEPENDENT ON OTHERS

Individuals who develop this terribly uncomfortable and limiting condition find themselves becoming more and more dependent on others, making more and more excuses for avoiding things. Most find their self-confidence dwindling to zero and, as a result, their self-esteem plummets, too. It is exciting for us to hear from those who have begun to turn that around:

You're right! Everyone does have her own pattern of resistance, learning, relaxing, tensing, changing. I started CHAANGE a year ago, September 1.
Let me tell you the most important thing that has happened to me! I like myself more. I was hugging myself the other night in bed. I used to hate myself for being worry-filled, tense, tired, not "able" to keep up with others. Now I just consider my ability to have gone through all that hell as <u>wonderful!!</u> And, it helps me appreciate others more. I tended to pity or be envious of others. Now, when I relax, I don't see things in the same light. I respect myself more, so I respect others more. I've got to respect myself - I'm such a neat person to have gone through what I went through and not have called "quits" and thrown myself in the river!
Thank you all a million times for your help! Every day I find new strengths in me - and, of course, that's where the strength lies.

And, the letter from a 34 year old women in another eastern state gives you some idea of the work involved in changing habits and attitudes:

...I'm so happy about myself that I'm not sure where to begin. Main important thing is while I may not be in total control of my life, I am in control of parts of my life and I know that I can be in control. Also I like myself. I am a good person.

On September eighth, I went out for the first time in three years and I felt good about it. Two of my children had to go to school for orientation. As we walked up to the school, I told myself that I was not crazy, not going to die, repeating, "I am getting better and will get over this!" As I got about a hundred steps away from the school, I really got panicky. I told my son to go on that I had to go home. I walked half way back home, stopped and really talked to myself, and then I turned around and went back to school. In school I looked into the auditorium and I really felt like running - instead I told myself that I should relax. I sat on the hall steps and did my relaxation exercise. Somewhere during the next two hours, my pains stopped. I couldn't even remember them stopping. I met new people and saw people that I haven't seen in three years. One teacher asked me where I have been keeping myself. Instead of lying to her I told her I have agoraphobia. God it felt good. I'm not ashamed of having agoraphobia. If people don't like it and can't understand it, that's their problem. I accept it and know that I can control it.

There are so many things in my life that have changed. My relationship with my husband. We can talk more openly with each other. When he gets angry and says something to me, I tell myself he's just blowing off steam and then I ask what's really happening. If I have done something then we sit down and talk it out. Before I ran to my room and cried. No more.

Even my children and I seem to get along better. My oldest daughter and I always seemed to be arguing about nothing. Whatever the problem was it always ended with both of us yelling. She ended up crying. I ended up with the attitude of 'what the heck.' Now we talk over the problem. If either of us start yelling we say to each other, "why are you yelling?" We really seem to be improving each other.

There are a lot of changes in my feelings about things. When I feel myself getting tense I repeat some of the sayings on the cards, tell myself I'm getting better, sing or think about something different. I used to keep myself on a very tight schedule. My housework had to be done at a certain time, kids had to have baths at a certain time – just about everything had to be done on time. No more, my housework gets done when I feel like doing it or my kids pitch in and help. I have more time for me. I read books, enjoy my family more. One of the changes that really amuses my husband is I finally have finger nails.

I play the weekly tape every day and the relaxation tape I play all day. My tapes arrive usually on Fridays. On Saturday I sit down and listen to my new tape and work with the workbook. On Sundays I get up a little early, play all my tapes and read all the literature that I have....

CREATING AN
ATMOSPHERE
FOR HELP

AREAS COVERED

The areas covered during the fifteen weeks include such things as commitment, relaxation, body signals, goals, habits, defenses, anger, responsibility, rights, choice, resistance, productive vs. nonproductive "dialogue," behavior changes, assertiveness, controlling oneself vs. controlling others, changes in one's "system," and gradual desensitization. Everything in the program is purposefully developed with one goal in mind: to help persons suffering with the agoraphobic condition learn to stop frightening themselves and become in control of their lives again. We know, without question, that once a person is able to do that, he/she is over agoraphobia.

Following are letters which relate to some of these specific areas:

From Ohio:

> ...*I feel that the last three days have been super for me. I babysat for my eight month old grandaughter Friday (stress!!!) I worked at a Church Bazaar in a <u>very</u> crowded shopping mall on Saturday, and today, Easter, I attended a breakfast and Church services with my family. I believe that the reason for my recent successes is that I have finally been able to accept, to a certain degree, the fact that I do have agoraphobia and that I may have certain panicky feelings or even panic attacks while I'm out. It wasn't until I went, with that thought in mind, actually experienced the panic in the grocery store, shopping mall and Church, that I attained some measure of confidence. Now, when I am asked to do something, or even think about doing, I'm able to dialogue with myself, "yes, you probably will experience some uncomfortable feelings, but breathe in and out slowly, relax and distract yourself."*
> *Today, I finally realized the connection between bodily reactions and panicky feelings, and*

was able to tell myself, "you're frightening yourself, you do have a choice, is this the one you want to go with?" It hit me as being so absurd, that I would choose to frighten myself and make myself feel absolutely terrible, that I was able to relax and let go. I finally believe, I guess, that it really is true, all those things you tell me on tape and in letters. The after feelings, that don't completely go away, the fogginess in my head, the heightened awareness to light and sound, I guess I didn't want to believe that I was like that, that those things really could bother me to such a degree, but they sure do! I feel more successful after having seen a panic attack through, than in going somewhere with no panic! I can't imagine that I'll never feel panicky again. It's been such a part of my life for most all my life to one degree or another.

"JUST DO IT"

The last psychologist that I went to (last time was Nov. '81) often told me, "stop thinking about it and just do it," pertaining to most things. Basically, I guess he was on the right track. It's been one of the hardest things I've ever had to do, to stop my mind from going in one direction and completely reverse it. Even with the tapes, I can do the muscle relaxation just fine, but disciplining myself to concentrate on the Imagery tape is really difficult. I never realized my total lack of concentration. It shows up in many areas, one being that I'm not a good listener, although I appear to be, people always think they have my undivided attention, when actually, nothing could be farther from the truth, I'm too busy worrying about their reaction to me, to listen.

I really needed to hear tape #7 and to read the information. It was a definite pep talk and a heavy decision for me. At first I was a little angry, I wanted someone to sympathize I guess, but then I realized, "gee, I can do that just fine all on my own." And I also was very reassured some-

*how, to finally believe that you really do care -
about me, my condition, my time and whether or
not I'm wasting my money.*

*Somehow, since I've been in the program,
my self esteem has risen quite a bit.   I'm able to
care more about me and my feelings without feeling
so selfish or guilty.   But it's a very fine line and
it's not clear enough in my mind for me to elaborate
on.*

*It's been unreal the way I've been able to
identify, probably 98% with Ann and Faison.   And
to know that there are really other people, just
like me, and they're intelligent, sensitive, etc. is
turning my life around in a positive direction.*

*I used to go way up and then way down,
until a couple of months ago, and I think the ways
up were, maybe, false hope.   I haven't gotten absolutely hopeful and exhilarated for quite a long time.
I do know, that this time, in this program, as I've
worked, and tested and tried, harder than I've ever
had to work at anything in my life, because this
is my life, there has been a very slow, gradual build-
up of hope (real) and most, important to me, confidence.   Maybe I am feeling more in control of my
life than I realize....*

From Michigan:

*The best part of the program is how I feel.
Knowing everything isn't in my head.
No more depression.
No more backaches.
No more shaky stomach.
No more bowel trouble.
No weird thoughts.
Going to bed and going to sleep within 10 to 15
minutes.
No worrying.
and probably alot more if I thought longer....*

LET GO

From New York:

....Well I don't know what is in your tapes, but I haven't felt like this in 12 years. I am so happy and everyone sees the change. It's hard to remember all the things you suggest doing but I've latched on to a few and it's wonderful.

I've "let go" worrying about my condition. I rest when tired. I've always had headaches, but they are under control. I've always dreaded vacations since my first attack started when I was away. Now I realize it was my doctor that I was afraid to be away from and I am now planning a trip to Hawaii. I may have to pack my tapes, but that's okay.

Thanks a million....

From North Carolina:

A couple of weeks ago, you asked me to write how I felt I was getting along. To be perfectly honest, the agoraphobic condition has so slipped from my mind, and we had houseguests, that only today did I realize I had not responded.

It has been a long time, since last Fall, that I had a severe attack. I still have some momentary anxieties, but now that I know how to relax and distract myself I can fight them off. I no longer worry about things in the future, feeling that I'll at least wait until the event occurs. For example, I was worrying about trips <u>way</u> in our future, how I would get on the plane, cross the bridge, go through the tunnel, etc.

It has been hard to change my lifestyle being isolated in the country with bad roads, but spring should be here shortly. I have worked hard at changing my attitude here, however. Yesterday was a most dreadful day weatherwise but instead of being blue, I forced myself to keep busy and happy, cooking

33

a special gourmet type dinner, getting out a cruise brochure, doing needlepoint. The day went by beautifully!

About the eleventh week I was feeling so assured that I kept pushing too hard and had a bit of a relapse. But I took to heart your message to take it easy and just let the changes come and that helped immeasurably.

I will write "my story" soon, but even that, and all the stress and sadness that brought this about, has just about left my consciousness. I think about it hardly at all, sometimes laugh at some of the aspects and at least am able to "plop it in a bucket" if it tries to once again haunt me.

My biggest remaining problem is driving alone - there again our bad road conditions have not helped. But spring will take care of that.

Your program has opened a wonderful new life for me and I am deeply grateful. My husband is so happy and has noticed the changes. He is 100% supportive at all times.

Thank you!

P.S. I will now take this across the road to the mailbox. In December, I couldn't cross the road!

RELAXATION

From West Virginia:

....The relaxation skills have been very helpful for me. One of my big fears is being on an interstate highway. Two weekends ago, I had a dinner date and decided to practice my relaxation skills before that evening and actually ride across the interstate bridge with my father driving. I was surprised at how relaxed I was, so that evening I rode in my date's car across the bridge to the restaurant. Of course, he had no idea of my problem as it was a blind date, another accomplishment for me as my social life has suffered over the last nine years due to my agoraphobia. It was a disappointing evening with my date, but a very successful evening practicing the behavior skills I'm learning in CHAANGE. I felt more relaxed and therefore was more able to be myself.

I also am fearful of driving on snow covered roads, the fear is "getting trapped," not an accident as most people feel. However, the past week I ventured out one morning on the icy roads and also was again surprised at how relaxed I was; I was the first one to get to work when in the past I stayed home.

It has been difficult during the Christmas season to do all the homework each week. However, I do make time for it and it is helping because even though I am very busy, I don't feel tense and rushed and try to listen to my body signals more carefully.

I am so thankful for your help. I only pray that I will continue to do as you say and use the positive thoughts so that some day soon I will be free of this condition....

BEHAVIOR PATTERNS

From California:

Last month I took a joyous vacation to Hawaii (including three flights each way) which I considered my graduation from all these lessons I've been learning! Something I never could have done a year ago! Out of fear of not feeling in control! I know that's behind me now. Each session didn't seem that important, but somehow the information, relaxing and understanding of my wrong behavior patterns had a cumulative effect. I felt I was taking the pressure off myself somehow. I knew I was starting to feel different inside, but my friends and family really notice the change. It's so nice to feel relaxed at being yourself!

I'm doing many things I didn't feel at ease with doing before, which lets me get beyond worrying about my physical self. I've handled _many_ driving situations now that easily could have overstressed

35

me before - it was my biggest problem. Now when I feel tension starting, I can reverse the feeling. My biggest aids are relaxing the hands (remembering that 'if the hands are relaxed, the body is relaxed'), saying to myself, "wrong computer input to the brain" when frightening thoughts start up, distracting myself right away with thoughts of activities and goals I had going for me and thinking about what good things happened to me that day. I also found the books very helpful. How I hope everyone who has gone through painful experiences like I had hears about you!!....

From Florida:

...The relaxation tape has helped me so much. Many days I have not been able to work in all of the times I was supposed to but I have really done the best I can with what time I have. I don't do well on it at night because I fall asleep I get so relaxed.

I get up early in the morning (2 hours before I go to work) and do the tape 5 times and then I walk a mile and a half and then get ready to go to work. I took the suggestion of a well planned exercise program and added the vitamins suggested to the ones I have already been taking. I have cut out the caffeine and sugar and I cannot tell you how much better I feel physically. No more tense muscles, especially the churning in my stomach. I would never have believed after 29 years that this could happen and I am delighted.

I still have some hang-ups and I was worried about that until the last tape came and you said if we didn't finish in the time allowed we should just go on and that is what I intend to do if I am not comfortable with everything at the end of the fifteen weeks.

I can drive or go anywhere I want comfortably now as long as someone is with me. I still have problems driving alone and shopping alone, but other than that I feel I have overcome so many things and for that I am very happy.

All I can say is thanks a million to you and your staff for this great program. After 29 years and several thousands of dollars in doctor's bills and still no help I feel I have really hit the "jack-pot" this time....

From Ohio:

....I've been in the CHAANGE program six weeks.

I just started my sixth week and to think I feel this good and positive and I'm not even half of the way through the program yet!

My main "fear" is (was) driving and shopping.

Last week we, my husband and I, had to take our son to the doctor - on the other side of town. I had decided early in the day that I was going to drive so I was, of course, thinking about it all morning. I handed the baby to my husband and said, "I'm driving - you won't be available always to go with me - so no time like the present to see if what I've learned so far will work!!" SUCH GUTS!!

I got in the car, drove toward the expressway (I haven't driven on that thing in four years!), and away we went!

What a sight! Me doing the breathing exercise (I was so scared) and my husband not looking too terribly comfortable - ha ha.

BRAVE WOMAN

Bridges are not #1 on my list of places to be - but when I approached it I was not as scared as I thought I'd be. When I got in the middle of the bridge I got cocky and turned my head and actually looked down at the water! (Brave woman!!)

Coming home I took a different "route" and was actually half way over the other bridge before I realized where I was. I had distracted myself by talking about what the doctor had said, etc. What a wonderful feeling!

Later in the week I was going to visit a friend and I usually take the long "safe" way to her house to avoid the expressway. Not so this time -- before I had time to even be anxious about it -- I headed for the on ramp and away I went. When I got there I excused myself to use the phone and called my husband to tell him of my accomplishment. He was as thrilled as I. Coming home I did it again - it was such a little "trip" but made me feel so good.

To date - Tape #6 is the BEST!!

Ann, I can really relate to you and what you're saying - especially when you mentioned thinking about "the route" while sitting in a chair before you even left the house! How true.

Also working up an argument before falling asleep at night. I've had some very interesting, one-sided mental fights -- how unproductive!

Do you know I've actually awakened in the morning mad at my husband from thinking "negative" thoughts before falling to sleep the night before. Poor fellow - the man has the patience of a saint!

I'm rambling, but it feels so good. Things are starting to fall into place for me -- my life and new skills.

I've got a new little one now and I don't have time for anything negative. What a wonderful time in my life to be introduced to CHAANGE.

Speaking of CHAANGE - when Lou says change she really means it doesn't she?

While getting dressed this morning I had to chuckle (out loud) about her comment on changing my order of putting the clothes on. I'm so glad your program has humor in it!

Many thanks for what you've taught me thus far....

From Oregon (with envelope marked 'success enclosed'!):

I couldn't wait for the tape to end this week (#11) after I played it for the first time because I

38

just had to share this super success with you both.

In the past I would try to do things as easily and simply as I possibly could because my negative thinking would cause me to be so depressed and exhausted that I could rarely function. Well, yesterday my daughter (14 mo.) was getting sicker after having had a bad cold for 4 days. I had to take her into the doctor. I was into the second day of a bad cold myself and I was achey all over and wanted to be in bed, our bathroom sink was plugged, and I had to call the roto-rooter man. Thus my day started.

I got up and said, "I'm going to enjoy this day, and have a good day. I want to take my daughter to the doctor to get some medicine. I give myself permission to be sick. This is life, it's the way things go. Everything will be okay." Well, we got to the doctor, he was 40 minutes late, we went to the pharmacy to get medicine, and they didn't have one of them so we piled into the car, my son also, and drove to another pharmacy, couldn't find a space to park, finally found one, got medicine, got home, lunch, naps, she was too fussy, I wanted to rest too but unable to because she would't sleep, so all up again. My son wanting someone to play over, me afraid to let anyone come, I took a risk for some new behavior and let him go next door (a new more productive behavior for me). My daughter finally down about 4:00 and roto-rooter man comes, after 1-1/4 hours it is done.

This whole time feeling sick and with a sick child, I did not get depressed! I did not wipe out with exhaustion! I even started a sewing project for fun and finished it and made a good dinner for my husband, the first in about a week. I gave myself permission to leave the dishes undone and was able to enjoy reading to my son before bed and we cleaned toys up together. I wasn't too tired and I was happy!

I can't tell you how different I am. My husband notices it and so does my son. I am so much happier and more easy going. I am letting go of controlling my son and his friends and am comfortable when he plays with them, letting him play with more children

- even ones I don't like too much! I am starting to allow myself to be sick and to take naps when I'm tired. The best part is that I am accepting myself as I am and am learning to really like the person that God made me. I don't like to be real busy outside my home and I'm accepting that as o.k. for me. I don't want to be really involved with the church and that's o.k. too. I like to be by myself a lot and do creative things like sewing and painting and refinishing furniture. I accept these things as neat things about myself and really love them. I'm so glad that there aren't any perfect people, aren't you? I really am enjoying every day. I even enjoy doing laundry, folding it and putting it away. I love it. Isn't it wonderful?!

Here's to our new lives, free to be who we are!

THE NEED TO BE PERFECT

From Michigan:

...A thought on letting go of my need to control others just came into my mind. As I am discovering and realizing, I _can_ have control over _myself_. I do not need to have control over others. I can't begin to tell you the number of other 'eye-openers' I have experienced since I started the CHAANGE program. And I LOVE it!! I really enjoy learning new things and feel my life is so much richer for what I am learning.

The one letting go I really am struggling with is the need to be perfect. As you probably know I am far from perfect - but I have the problem with beating myself up mentally for things I feel it would be preferable to do. But I am working on it. Ask my family. More and more my response to any criticism from them is, "that's okay - don't you remember - I don't have to be perfect anymore?" You can't imagine the relief I felt when in week four, the homework was "to allow yourself permission to be less than 100% perfect this week." At last, I was given permission to relax my guard on myself - and what revelation I felt the first time I caught myself berating myself because I didn't go somewhere. I said to myself, "hey knock it off - don't you remember - you don't have to be perfect this week." What a relief!!

Also I need working on letting go of my panicky, scared feelings of being afraid. But if I didn't need to work on these, I wouldn't be in CHAANGE would I?

IT TAKES PERSISTENCE

From Indiana:

Just a note to let you know how I am getting on.

I can't tell you how happy I feel today. Two weeks ago we had a "movie party" in our basement and showed old movies to our friends. Although I still had a small amount of apprehension at Christmas time, I had none at this party. Next month, we're planning a potluck between parades for a bunch of old car friends, and I can hardly wait. Our home is situated between two small towns where the parades will be taking place, and we're the logical gathering place.

I'm sure you don't remember, but it was this identical parade party last year that gave me one whale of a set-back (not practice opportunity, believe me!). I called you in tears after that Sunday, and it threw me so much that I wanted to throw in the towel. I had my son's graduation party a couple of weeks later, and it was almost more than I could do to go on with it.

After about a week of moping and stewing around last year, I decided that the best thing to do was to begin again and get on with it. Of course, as soon as I got my attitude around, things began going better again. Nevertheless, I had just about decided that I would compromise with myself. Was entertaining really that important? I enjoyed going out lots more anyway.

I didn't compromise, and it got easier all of a sudden. I'm so thankful, and you can't believe what a high I've been on since our movie party. I told my husband that I was already beginning to plan the parade party, and what we'd have, etc. He immediately assumed that I was worried about it. How neat that I'm not.

Perseverance really pays off. Just like a beginning athlete, it takes lots and lots of persistence to improve and make the grade. It's a mistake to give up.

I really identified with the writer in the newsletter who worries. That's a hard habit to break. I even worried that something was wrong with me because I worried - stewing. It helped me to examine possibilities. My husband might be late because he was in an accident. But the more logical possibility was that he had to work overtime, etc. My habit was to sift out the most negative possibilities with no consideration to the positive. I've made fantastic strides in this area, and I'm a much happier person for it.

I've decided to do some writing. I always enjoyed doing letters to the editor and that sort of thing, but I never gave serious consideration to anything more because I never thought of "becoming" a writer, but only of "being" one, which I wasn't. And besides, it really wasn't a very "practical" goal anyway.

Anyhow, it's so much fun that I really don't care if I ever get very good. I'm doing it for myself. I find myself constantly thinking about what I will put down on paper next. I'm enclosing an article that I did for our local newspaper. I had a sure-fire subject, so I knew that it was not my expertise that got it published. However, I did get $15.00 for it.

My best to all of you.

NEW STANDARDS

From Pennsylvania:

I think #9 session turned a significant corner for me and #10 has shown me how significant.

1. Since I had improved my sphere of activity and reduced my avoidance to "the long trip," that "long trip" had become the gauge by which I judged my recovery from agoraphobia. I feel free to put that on hold believing that the day will come when I will want to do it and will. Besides it's getting so nice up here now, who needs to go to Florida?

2. After 4 years of agoraphobia I judged <u>everything</u> in my life -- feelings, actions, goals, work, pleasure, etc. by my agoraphobic standards. I am pulling the plug on that. It can go. I'm getting new standards by which to gauge the quality of my time. They are not nearly so tough on me.

3. Having succeeded before the program in reducing most of my avoiding I was hopeful that it would help me out of what I call the agoraphobic blahs - that crummy feeling carried around somewhere in one's mid-section. I've learned that the crummy feeling originates with crummy thoughts. Now I knew that! Why didn't I think that it applied here and to me!

4. I think I'm at the point where I realize that there is more to this than floating. I really do have a life that has been directed by negatives. It may have taken 40 years for those negatives to bring me into this condition, but I am beginning to see more clearly my own set of patterns that need to be replaced.

5. I've been using the rubberband on the wrist method of making myself aware of negative, non-productive thoughts or attitudes.

Again and again, thanks for such a clear and sensible program for recovery!

From Ohio:

...If you should ask me how I am doing I would answer, "I have a long way to go." However when

I look back I can't believe it! I made notes every week of "my condition" and I just re-read them. Did I really write these things? My notes are filled with phrases like, "extremely depressed," very nervous and tense," "a lot of anxiety" and "many panic attacks." I just don't remember feeling this badly!

At the top of my list of things I wanted to do again was grocery shopping. Now I can take time to read labels, compare prices and fill two carts. I do go at a time of day when the store is less crowded - a double benefit since I go through the checkout much faster. I can honestly say I can go into a grocery store with no anticipatory fears, as a matter of fact. I have forgotten the panic attacks that occured there. Hoorah!

Just before Christmas two of my children graduated from college. This meant going to two separate ceremonies - one hour apart, at a different location on campus. The first ceremony caused some discomfort but by the time the second got under way I was calm and relaxed (almost). My family was delighted that I could attend.

I haven't been shopping since Christmas - went three times before Christmas - one disaster and two very good experiences. I will try soon again but I have been too busy.

The stress I felt at work is becoming a "good" stress I think (I work better under pressure). The pressure is changing from "clenched jaw" tension to the normal pressures of the workload. I can even manage to relax at work now!

We went to the theater last weekend. I was hoping we would be early enough to avoid most of the sell-out crowd but this was not the case. I was uncomfortable at first. I will be going again next month and I know it will be better because I enjoy the theater and will be calm and relaxed.

I am working hard on negative thoughts and letting go. On to lesson 10!

P.S. On re-reading this I notice a lot of exclamation points but doggone it, I'm proud of my progress!...

44

CHANGING PATTERNS

From New York:

....*I was writing a few questions to you today, asking for answers, since I seem so harried all the time trying to fit in everything in a day. I suddenly realized ten minutes ago that that was my problem! That is what you mean on the tapes by changes in patterns.*

I'm doing all the tapes, all the homework, reading the books, trying to learn, and at the same time doing about everything I <u>ever</u> did, including cooking long, time-consuming dishes like soups and casseroles, etc.; reading four newspapers instead of one, watching baseball play-offs and World Series, taking care of ten animals, answering telephones, paying bills, and entertaining!!

I simply have not changed enough habits, and have too long a "should list." I surely am not as bright as you say most agoraphobics are. This piece of knowledge took seven sessions! ....

From Maryland:

I just wanted to drop you a note to let you know how I am getting along. A one-word description is GREAT!!

I used to go to a health/exercise club, but had to stop a while ago because I kept having panic/anxiety attacks while there. I have just started going back to the club, with only minor pangs of anxiety, which I am able to relax away. In fact, I'm so comfortable, I have signed up for a lifetime membership.

Also, I have a friend with whom I work every day, and she has always made me tense and anxious because of her outbursts of temper, screaming fits, etc. As a result I was always very anxious at work waiting for her to blow up, which happened on an average of 4-5 times a week. Of course, what I was

45

always really afraid of was that she might be mad at me (rejection), and you know how we people have to be "perfect." Anyway, I then started saying, "so what?", and what do you know, my anxiety has all but disappeared. Now that I have let go of the fear and anger I always felt towards her, I realize that I really enjoy her company and can appreciate all her good qualities - something I was never able to do before. I am so much more comfortable at work than I have ever been, and besides, it seems like I have a brand new friend. She hasn't changed any, but I have; and, it's TERRIFIC!!!

There are so many little things that I am able to do now. I am friendlier and more open with people than I was when I was trying to "hide" my condition; I am more relaxed and comfortable in everything I do; and, the best part is that now I am living, instead of just existing in my self-built "fear box." There's a new me, and I love her. Thanks.

CHANGE
HAS NO
BOUNDARIES

REVOLUTIONARY BREAK-THROUGH

We consider the taped therapeutic program a revolutionary break-through in delivery of health services. Although there are many informational tapes available, we know of no other therapeutic process on tapes. At this time, those of us affiliated with CHAANGE have worked with over 2000 people who were sufferers of agoraphobia. CHAANGE tape clients have been from each state, plus Canada, Mexico, Brazil, Puerto Rico, France, Switzerland, the Republic of China, Germany and the Virgin Islands. Statistically, the average age of those with whom we have worked is 40.3, with range of age 15 to 82. 72% are women, and 28% men. An amazing 66% had been in treatment prior to their participation in the CHAANGE program, many over many years and with several different therapists. The average age at onset is 29, and the average number of years suffered is 13 years. The range of years suffered is from 3 months to 54 years. Incapacities range from minor - such as unable to give a speech - to a person's being totally housebound for many years. Interestingly, 53% of the CHAANGE participants were taking mood-altering drugs when they began the program, while only 10% were still taking them at completion. We asked people to rate the amount of control they felt of their life on a scale of 0 (none) to 10 (total control). At the start of the fifteen week program, the average was 3.4, and at completion, 7.9.

OLDER PEOPLE CHANGE TOO

I think the letters that thrill me the most are from those who are in their sixties and seventies - people who have felt they would never again have the freedom they so want to experience.

This from a 67 year old man from Delaware:

Completed my tape program three weeks ago but have procrastinated about writing to you.

Four months ago (before CHAANGE) I had gotten as far as I could go on my own. I could drive alone but not too far, could go in small stores, restaurants - if I sat near an exit - anything I did I had to have an escape route nearby. I had learned that I had agoraphobia but didn't have the skills to cope with it.

After finishing the CHAANGE tape program here is where I am: can drive alone for greater distances, can go in large stores now although the large enclosed malls still give me some trouble. I wondered if each store would have to be conquered separately but I find that overcoming the fear of one store helps you in all the others. Restaurants pose no problem. Walking around the small town where I live gives me the greatest pleasure because for many years I could not do that. There are many other things I can do now - I won't list them but they are important to me.

As you have probably gathered I live in a rural section. How I could cope with the "big city" I don't know. Perhaps I don't even want to. I don't have to anyway.

One more thought. Why don't clinics, etc. for the treatment of agoraphobia advertise? For years I never heard the word agoraphobia, much less a treatment for it. It was just by chance that I read the article on agoraphobia in Better Homes and Gardens and decided to send for information (one of the better decisions of my life). Just recently I discovered from a local newspaper article that a doctor - just twelve miles from my home - treats agoraphobics. Has been for 4 or 5 years but it was a well kept secret. I would gladly tell people about CHAANGE if I knew who the people needing help were.

In conclusion, let me say that doing things that were a problem several months ago are now easy. I hope that as I continue to do more and more things eventually I won't have to even think about them and agoraphobia will be just a memory.

We are very aware of the "big secret" of agoraphobia which is the major reason we try hard to do television and radio shows to let people know there is hope.

This is from a 68 year old woman:

...As you know I am a older person "68," which is quite old to change my ways of living. I feel that there have been lots of changes in me as I look back when I first started the program in December.

My nerves are so much better. I can control myself so much better. My family think I am much more relaxed. I like to think I can float through my panicky and scared feeling pretty well also.

I am trying my new skills and know I will make it a little at a time.

I want to thank you and all the fine people connected with the program. It is a life saving miracle that I never expected to find. I will use it for the rest of my life....

RECENTLY WIDOWED

A 66 year old woman:

First of all, I am 66, have suffered from this condition since 1979, recently lost my husband of 40 years, and have two adult children (both successful) and worked for 42 years. At the time of my retirement I was an administrative assistant to a dean of a professional school at a University.

I have reviewed the first listing of my incapacities and limitations which numbered 13 (all very severe) and was absolutely amazed to discover I am now doing nine of these with little or no anxiety, and two with mild anxiety. This leaves only two situations which are still very difficult and even these have lessened somewhat. Needless to say, I am filled with joy over this improvement. I wish I had someone with which to share this happy progress, but I have kept my condition to myself, never discussing it with even my husband, son or daughter. The reason I did not tell my husband is because his own health was very poor and he was dependent upon me. I could not bring myself to add to his burden, however I am sure that

50

had he known he would have understood and given me his support. Somehow I was able to function so that he never once hinted that he noticed I was having difficulties. But, believe me, every day for two years I felt like I was climbing mountains all day long. After seven sessions of counseling with a minister-psychologist for panic, I did improve somewhat. During the last two months of my husband's life there were times I felt so well that I even suggested that we eat out for a change (eating out was #1 limitation). I had no difficulty in coping with the emergency of getting my husband to the hospital, talking to the doctors, being with him for two days before his death....nor any difficulty in making the funeral arrangements including arranging for 100 (plus or minus) guests to be invited to my home afterwards. I also had no difficulty in attending to the many necessary details regarding our business affairs. However, when friends began inviting me to luncheons and dinners, I began to get bad again. This, added to the grieving process, put me back to square one.

It was at this time that I heard Ann and Faison on the local news talk show. I was so anxious that I could hardly listen to them and kept turning the volume down so I wouldn't hear all they had to say, but then forced myself to turn the volume up near the end of the program so I could get your address. Even writing the letter to you requesting information, reading your printed information and listening to the introductory tape was very anxiety-producing. In fact, it was just awful.

Immediately upon receipt of tape #1 and the relaxation tape, I started to improve and have kept on improving. It is almost like a miracle. Not only has this agoraphobia condition improved, but I am convinced that my grief was lessened even more than it normally would have because of this program. Most days of this program I have felt improvement, but I did experience two really major backward steps that were very discouraging; it took me several weeks each time to climb back up again.

Most mornings I now awaken looking forward to the day. I spend three days of the week doing volunteer office work, a different assignment each day. Previously, I was doing just one day a week and almost no longer could do even that. All my life I have loved to entertain but had reached the point where the mere thought of it would cause an anxiety attack. Now I can have friends and family over for dinner with less effort than ever. I have a feeling that when I really completely overcome this condition, I will be better than I ever have been.

I still have a problem with fear-enhancing and worry thoughts; I still have anticipatory fear in some situations; but all of these "stills" have become better than they were. I recently sat down and just off the top of my head very quickly listed my improvements and "cans." I thought you might be interested in this list, remembering that each item represents a big improvement. This list is not prioritized, it is just as I thought of them.

The minister-psychologist whom I consulted understood my panic, but his method of treatment was in trying to find the cause which he attempted to do by regressive meditation. This did not work for me. However, he also gave me homework, reading material and affirmations which did help. So, when I became involved with your program, the homework and affirmations were not new to me.

I have five more weeks in this program and I know I will continue to improve and will overcome those last limitations. It is wonderful to know that I will always have the tapes and all of the reading material for reinforcement. Some day I may even have the courage to tell my son and daughter about this experience. Sometimes I think they should be told so that when or if anything happens to me and they find my binder and tapes they will not agonize over what their mother was experiencing.

And, a 62 year old woman:

> *Please tell the girls, Lou, Faison and Ann that since taking your course I am driving again, after 15 years. Maybe you don't think I am elated over this!*
>
> *I drive with someone with me and if I choose to, later I will take the car out alone. I have been helped a great deal - the tapes are almost too good to be true.*
>
> *Found my biggest hang-up was my slush fund of old angers. I have been harboring them for so many years it wasn't easy to let go of them.*
>
> *Heartfelt thanks to each and every one of you.*

KEY PROBLEMS

There were several key problems which had to be resolved as we began developing the therapeutic program on tapes. We had already addressed the original issue of how to respond to people all around the country by deciding to offer our treatment process on tapes. It is important to remember that, at that time, there were no appropriate referral sources to whom we could refer; so the dilemma was to either offer nothing, to offer to see people at the Center in groups, or to find a way to reach them where they were. We had ruled out the first and decided the second was impractical. A major concern was how we could be sure that the person with whom we worked "by tapes" actually suffers with agoraphobia and not something else. We solved that problem by the material we send out to them, by the way we present the condition when talking about it, and by the evaluation forms we send before the actual program materials arrive. The initial informational and descriptive brochure is filled with questions and answers that exclude other disorders, yet include agoraphobia. Included are many phrases, comments, and complaints of the "typical" agoraphobic when in therapy. So far, with the exception of one woman who came to one group session and then realized she was in the wrong place, no one has self-diagnosed this condition incorrectly. We do, however, have a small percentage of "dropouts" and there is certainly a good probability that most of these clients may have found the condition of agoraphobia not to be their problem.

MAKING THE PROGRAM SPECIFIC

So, our next obstacle was how to make the program specific and individual. We had found that there were amazing similarities in the background and in the personality of those who developed agoraphobia. We put this information to work by designing what we called our "Development of Agoraphobia" chart. In the first session, after a taped discussion of just what agoraphobia is and how it develops, we ask the client to follow along, shading in those boxes on the chart which are appropriate for him. We have found this to be the most important single element which helps participants feel that the program is individually and specifically tailored to them and their individual needs. Many people are astounded to find out that we 'know' them so well. For instance,

From California:

First of all, let me say that I look forward with great delight each week to hearing your soothing Southern voices and the common sense knowledge imparted on the tapes, always shared with humor in a warm, kind, designed-to-heal fashion. I suppose you've heard this time and time again but while I was busily shading in all the blocks in the chart - Development of Agoraphobia/Anxiety, I was stunned about how the autobiographical details of my life were there on that piece of paper - How could CHAANGE know all this!? Funny Magic........

I am in my ninth week and I can honestly say that in the eleven years I've been driving, only the last five or six weeks have I done so in a relaxed manner. I have also been going to the market with

54

*increasing frequency (comfortably), both successes
I attribute directly to your program...*

From Illinois:

*I started the CHAANGE program just two weeks
ago and I have learned more about my condition from
the materials and tapes I have received (especially
the Development of Agoraphobia chart), than I had
learned from all the books I had read and the more
than two years of on and off therapy.*

*After filling out the enclosed sheet I put it aside...
only to pick · it up several days ago to read what I
had written. I actually sat down and laughed! Seeing
my problems black on white showed me that I concern
myself with "what they will think of me." I know
that through your program I will change that to read,
"So what! I'm not perfect, I really don't care what
'they' might think!"*

*For years I had no idea of what those panicky
feelings were all about. I exhausted every book and/or
magazine article I could find, only to find that the
harder I'd try to get over agoraphobia by myself,
the more it seemed it reacted on me. To learn it's
a bodily response is a relief!*

*I am keeping a personal chart on how the tapes
are helping me. I am also writing my autobiography
pinpointing how I developed agoraphobia.*

*What a wonderful program you have developed!
I only wish I'd found you sooner!*

God bless you!

BEGINNING TO FEEL CONFIDENT

From Pennsylvania:

*I just wanted to drop a few lines now that I am
at the halfway point in your program. After having
inquired in several programs throughout the U.S. (they
were listed in an article in "Better Homes & Gardens")
I chose CHAANGE because I was so impressed with*

your sincerity in wanting to help; so many of the others just struck me as being interested in making money. I know that God led me in the right direction. When I play those tapes I just can't believe how well you know me! Your informality and the obvious friendship that exists between you and Ann and Faison in itself is very relaxing. I know you've heard this all before, but I've learned so much about myself and I feel confident that I will get over this.

I would also like to thank you for making yourselves so available. In the beginning of the program, I had an occasion to call Ann. It seems that I misunderstood about playing the relaxation tapes and was trying to play each side ten times. Needless to say, I was going nuts trying to find time to do this – I was just about ready to pack my bags and move in with my Mom until I was done with the program. Between my husband, housework, fulltime job, and dog, I knew I'd have to give one up temporarily to get through the program. Luckily, I remembered the number you gave to call Ann. She was delightful; I felt I always knew her - luckily she set me straight fast.

When I get over this, I'd like to help in some way; but I'm afraid it would just contribute to my problem of never taking time out for myself. But I just can't thank you enough for everything.

From Missouri:

In the 10th week of the course you asked that we let you know how we were coming along. I didn't know what to say, for I really wasn't sure. It seemed like I was becoming anxious about more things than I had been in awhile. I was reassured quite a bit though when I read that this was quite normal since I was nearing the end of the program. I had kept telling myself this but reading it from you really helped to ease my mind.

I am constantly amazed at how you always seem to answer the questions that I am having on the tapes that you send. I'll be thinking about something and then I'll receive the tape for the week. Lo and behold, the question or questions I've been wondering about are answered. In the beginning of the program, I was a bit leery and I know that my family and friends wondered how a taped program could work, with no one right there to ask questions to. But it does and I'll never be able to thank you enough for how you have helped me.

The week that I sent away to start the CHAANGE program I was put into contact with an agoraphobic group here. They wanted me to join the group they were starting. I was tempted, but felt that I had finally committed myself to something and would give it a try. I felt that if your program didn't work, I could always start with theirs later. I'm so glad I did. The counselor that they hired, who was supposed to be familiar with agoraphobics, figured she had taught them all she could after only one meeting a week for six weeks. She is gone now, and they are once again a lost group of people with nowhere to turn. I hope that they will turn to CHAANGE.

One more thing - tape #11 and Faison were so helpful. Remember how she went to a strange town and had lunch with her cousin? Well, my husband's boss offered his employees and their wives a CPR course. My husband and I signed up, but I was really scared about the whole situation. I had never met any of the people where he worked and the course was a 6-hour affair. Listening to how you and Faison said that any new situation caused one to be anxious helped me to get there. Like Faison, I had a few thoughts during the hours in that building, but I quickly put them aside. I had prepared myself to even walk out during the program if need be. Now the good part - I didn't need or want to and am now qualified to help someone if the occasion arises. I'm so proud of my card that they gave to me at the end of the program. I was even the first volunteer to practice the method on the dummy. Never in my life have I been the first to speak up. Everyone was happy at the end of the course, but I felt like I was going to simply explode with happiness with what I had accomplished. Being in buildings was a problem for me, but no more.

Thank you so much for your help and understanding....

From Texas:

Well, I decided not to wait to write my progress report until I am "perfectly" over this condition...I'm beginning to realize that I'm pretty much stuck with "me" - the good part is, that doesn't seem so bad anymore.

POSITIVE CHANGES

I've had agoraphobia/anxiety for the last 8 years and before that was subject to fairly severe depressions since I was 19 (I'm almost 35 now). I'd been to psychiatrists, psychologists and counselors and was sort of "addicted" to them - when I quit I'd get more depressed or panicky. I took Librium off and on for 8 years to help with the anxiety.

I'm married with children and my driving phobia started when I was about to get laid off from a job. I didn't get laid off and drove to and from work for the next several years with varying degrees of panic and fairly severe anxiety at work as well as on the road. For the last 5 years off and on I worked on a Master's degree (which will be awarded in May). I've read books, studied cognitive psych., behaviorism, understand Freud's theories and have even done some relaxation and biofeedback. None of the above "cured" my agoraphobia. I went to meetings for a year or so and the actual practice and positive self-statements helped me probably more than anything else I'd tried, but the contact with "former mental patients" scared me and then I'd feel guilty for feeling that way. I also had a hard time with their "lingo," angry temper, etc. and got down on myself for feeling superior or trying to be an intellectual. What I wanted was something like that - only updated - incorporating the best of the _new_ knowledge while not throwing out the best of the old. CHAANGE is that way.

One of the first positive changes I noticed (after only 4 weeks) was that I was doing things I had done with a lot of anxiety with less anxiety so that instead of feeling like "I'm glad I got through that," I was actually not dreading doing it again, which led to less overall anticipatory anxious feelings and some reduction in my ruminations about being a person "who can't even enjoy things which _should_ be pleasurable."

I stopped the Librium after a few weeks of relaxation training.

My "presenting" problem was fear of driving - particularly on the freeways or with anyone in the car with me, but part of the function this served was to keep me cut off from people, so actually the biggest problem was loneliness. My shaky self-esteem just couldn't take people finding out about my problem and thinking me weird, or worse, "crazy." The crazy thing is a big one with me. My mother spent a year or two in a mental hospital after a nervous breakdown - my parents were divorced at the time and I ended up living with my father. There was a lot of fear and mystery surrounding her illness. I was there when she "broke down" - all she did was start crying, but they whisked her away and I only saw her once (in the hospital) after that for the next 21 years. I wrote and talked on the phone, but didn't see her (which I felt terribly guilty about). I think maybe down deep I've had a terrible fear that if I "broke down" someone would "whisk me away" from my family. I've tried to be a perfect parent and could never tolerate any criticism about my "parenting."

SETS SELF UP

Since starting the CHAANGE program, I've become much more aware of how I set myself up and instead of blaming others for my problems I'm learning how to stop setting myself up, how to ask for help. I'm more assertive with my husband and children. I'm *realizing that people have stayed away from me not because I'm an icky person, but because sometimes I've manipulated the situation so that they won't want to be around me, and I'm starting to stop beating on myself for doing this - realizing that it's defensive behavior that I used because I didn't know what else to do. You can't really begin to tear down some of your defenses until you think it might be safe to come out from behind them. I especially like the way your program is structured because the initial emphasis on relaxation, i.e. learning a positive new skill, made me feel like I had something to "fall back on" - a core of strength at a time when I had serious doubts about there being anything strong at my core - this isn't put very well but I hope you can get the gist of what I'm saying.*

Hearing Ann and Faison on the tapes talking about many of the same foibles and fears I've had has been invaluable in helping me realize that craziness and having problems are two different things and that asking for help does not mean one is on the verge of falling apart. It has also helped tremendously with my terrible feelings of loneliness and isolation. Hearing the three of you on the tapes has been like having three friends....

Working hand in hand with one's ability to self-diagnose this condition, is the fact that nearly all persons who have had agoraphobia for any length of time have been to physician after physician, specialist after specialist, trying to find help. Many have been mis-diagnosed and mistreated which, of course, compounds the problem. It is not unusual for a client to have seen ten doctors, to have seen several psychiatrists and other therapists. Some have even been hospitalized and given electric shock treatments. We recommend to the clients that they make sure their physician has ruled out those conditions in which symptoms can be similar - e.g., hypoglycemia, hyperthroidism, inner-ear disturbances, etc., and our medical/psychiatric consultant is used whenever there is a question regarding a medical problem. Our focus is on helping the person learn to stop frightening himself <u>about</u> his symptoms which are caused by anxiety.

THE PRIDE OF SUCCESS

Such was the case with this mother:

...My youngest son is getting married March 13 and I have had lots of planning and showers to attend. This wedding is what really made my decision to call CHAANGE. I did not know how I was going to sit in front of that church during the wedding. Want you to know that I am now looking forward to it. Have been to showers or different parties for bride-to-be. One was all the way across town without my husband or daughter to be with me, but went with daughter-in-law and a neighbor - had one tense moment but got right over it. Then went to one at sister's house with no problem, another at my house, and the one that I was proudest of was my husband took me to a house and put me out and left. It was at a home where I did not know anyone but bride-to-be and her Mother. I had no panicky feelings, was very pleased with myself. When this wedding is over I plan to let you know that I marched down that aisle with my head high and sat comfortably during whole ceremony.

One week later we received this note:

...Well, the big day has come and gone and thanks to CHAANGE I marched down that long aisle with my head high and sat through the wedding without much fear or anxiety but knew there would be some emotional feelings but was able to handle them all. It was very emotional to me because it was our baby and last child to be married and all the other children and small grandchildren were in the wedding party. Also went to bridesmaid luncheon on Friday and was hostess at rehearsal dinner on Friday night for 44 people and came through with flying colors. Husband

and children were very proud of me and I was very pleased with myself for having had the nerve to call CHAANGE and enlist in your program. I know I have a long way to go yet, but am glad to be where I am today....

and, from South Carolina:

Preferably, this letter would be addressed to all who work at CHAANGE because I'd like to share my success and joy in learning with each and every one.

Today I rec'd Tape #5. I marvel continually at the progress I've made throughout the last five weeks.

For the last three weeks I've been attending church (hadn't been since last Easter) -- it's a different church than I used to attend, but nevertheless it is a church where my children and I all feel very comfortable and look forward to going two nights a week and on Sundays.

Twice I've driven to a nearby town (45 miles) for the first time in a year to visit close friends (I'd not driven at all for about four months).

I have been grocery shopping, to restaurants, have found I could get through uncomfortable feelings in a very short period of time and actually enjoy myself. It'd been 8 mos. since I'd shopped.

FORGOT VOW MADE

My step-father was in the C.C. Unit in our very largest hospital this week. I forgot the vow I'd made to myself last August, that "I'll never ever go there again!" Practiced breathing exercises on the elevator and in corridors - did a few knee-bends here & there - before long I found I was able to reach out and comfort another lady in the waiting room. THAT'S PROGRESS, FOLKS!

Truthfully, I can say I have a new lease on life - a new relief and reward every day and that fantastic release from fear.

My doctor is now helping me decrease the medication and I hope soon to have these muscles relaxed all by myself.

Needless to say, my family is OVERJOYED. We're beginning to find FUN a part of our lives again, even amidst the trials of the times.

From Indiana:

Things are beginning to come together a little for me. After listening to session #8, I decided "why not go for a drive." I took my 18 yr. old son with me. We were just going around the square mile, but after we drove awhile, I decided to go to town about 5 miles away. I was a little anxious when I first got to town, even though it is only a small town (8,000 or so). With some dialogue the moment passed. I then decided to see if I could get my hair cut at a small beauty shop. She is never too busy, and my hair had not been cut since last November. I had to wait about 20 minutes. The point of all this is that I made it through the ordeal. I cannot say that it was totally anxiety-free, but as I sat there, I repeated my dialogues, and I relaxed. It's a totally different feeling and experience for me. I was in there for 40 minutes or so (a record for me) without getting up and running out. I had given up everything except going to the grocery or some stores (always with my husband or son). I can now manage these places with their help with very little anxious feelings.

I AM GETTING BETTER

If I do get anxious, I use "I am getting better and I will get over this." In fact, I'm wearing it out by using it so much. I can go into the stores by myself as long as it's only for a few items at a time and only when they're not so busy (lines really tend to upset me).

I still get anxious before trying the other things I used to do or even just thinking about them, but at least the anxiety doesn't last as long or take control of me as it used to. I used to worry for a week before an event took place. Now I can feel myself relaxing more since I started this program...

When my agoraphobic condition started about four years ago, I also found out I had severe anemia which I still doctor for with B-12 shots and vitamins. Since both came at about the same time, I really didn't have any energy. Each was draining me. I would work for 5 minutes and rest for an hour. It was awful. Now that I am working on both conditions at once, I do have more energy and am using that energy to work on the agoraphobia...Meanwhile I will continue with lesson #8. Onward and upward! I am spending more time with my tapes, hoping to be ready for my son's graduation and confirmation in May – also one son's last concert. My major housework will have to wait until mid-summer. Thanks so much for helping me get this far. As my attitude changes, so do I...

P.S. I was in a state of anxiety most of the time when I first started the program (due to thinking about the agoraphobia and really not knowing what to expect or what was expected of me). Now I have settled down considerably and it is working for me because I am working with the program.

From North Carolina:

...My condition really started at about 12 years of age. One night I thought I had overeaten so I proceeded to take aspirin to relieve my stomach-ache. That was not enough for me so I also took some baking soda. I really don't remember just what all I took. Well, naturally I felt a little funny. Then I began to think I had taken too much and was going to die. My daddy got up out of bed and took me to the doctor. I can remember it so well - I felt that I was going to die every step of the way. When we arrived at the doctor's office I ran in and told him that I felt

I had gas around my heart. He looked at my daddy and then gave me a shot. Immediately I was fine. I think now that I probably had the perfect person in my mind and felt that what he had given me saved my life. I never had another panic attack until I was 20 years old. Again it was connected with medication. I was now grown, married, and working a job. I had been nervous and the doctor had given me some phenobarbital. That particular morning I was going in early to ask my boss for a raise. You see I have never been a person to wait and if they eventually thought that I deserved a raise, give me one. I had been with the company a year. I knew I was doing a good job or they would have told me so. In my mind I felt that they felt I was satisfied with my salary so why pay me more. A lot of companies and even people are like that, you know. Well, I decided that if one pill made me at ease, two would surely put me more at ease. And I have to tell you that that morning I was just plain scared. Well, I took the two pills and went off to work. About half way there I began to feel very strange. I immediately thought I had overdone it again and that, in turn, scared me. I thought I would surely die. I promised myself that if I could make it to town, I would go to the hospital and tell them what I had done. Surely they would be able to do something. I made it O.K. and somehow, by the time I reached town, I had gotten myself somewhat in control. I did not go to the hospital. That would have been silly to tell them what I had done. I thought I was O.K. once again, but this time I did not get by as lightly as the first. Every morning, as I would start to town, at about the same spot that I had the panic attack the morning I had taken the pills, I would have another attack. I went to the doctor and felt quite silly trying to explain what my trouble was, because after I reached the stop light in town, I would be quite alright. I can't tell you how I overcame this, but I did. It only lasted a couple of weeks. My third time was the big one for me. I was 31 years old by then, with several children. My husband was involved with another woman and the previous night

I had caught him with her. This had been going on for about a year. I had gotten to where I had real bad headaches every day. It seemed as if I got up with them and went to bed with them. I now know from you that I was under a lot of stress. I didn't even know that then. I didn't know anything about body signals. My youngest child at this time was only 4 months old. That morning I got up with a terrible headache. I took a capsule that my doctor had prescribed for me. All I had on my mind was what was happening in my marriage. I took another capsule, forgetting I had already taken one, and went to make up the bed. I was O.K. until I remembered I had taken one before. I immediately went into panic thinking I would surely die. I called the doctor and the nurse answered. I told her what I had done. She told me she would have the doctor call me back. Well, I was in bad shape and that was not good enough for me. I was by this time in the grip of a full-fledged panic attack. I put the children in the car and drove 10 miles to the doctor's office. He sat me down, gave me something to make me throw up and talked to me. When I left his office, I was fine. This happened in about May. I did not have another panic attack until October. Then I would have one about every two weeks, each time being O.K. once they were over with. The 21st day of December 1971, I had gone to the beauty shop in town and was on my way home, when a panic attack hit me, and from then on I was in the what I now know was the spiral deal. My question is, Lou, why did I take so long? I really must be a hard-headed person. That is what my doctor laughingly told me. He has been the best person to me. He did everything in his power to help me. He even checked your firm out, if you remember, before he would allow me to take the treatment.

STILL WAITING

Today I am in my 13th week of treatment. I still have not gotten completely over this condition, as I wrote you last week when I had the panic attack, but I am a lot better. I am still waiting for that something, and I don't know what, that will put it all together for me. And I really believe it will happen. Today I went to Sunday School and Lou, I really must tell you that that is one of the shoulds that I cannot give up. I was scared, but I went telling myself all the while I could do it. I dialogued and relaxed the whole time. I even told myself that of course you are going to be anxious - anybody would be. I told myself that I wasn't going to view it as anxiety, I was going to view it as excitement. Lou, if they could have read my mind, they would have called the men in the white coats and had me committed today, for everyone would have thought I was mad. I did not stay for church. I had had success in Sunday School and I didn't want to overdo the first time. I don't know how I will react next time, but I really felt good that I had gone to Sunday School and had a success. I know I am not out of the woods, but at least I can begin to see daylight, and that is a lot.

UNNECESSARY SHOULDS

From Texas:

I was going to wait until I got some pretty stationery before I wrote to you, but that's an old "should" isn't it and one I no longer need. I know you will be just as interested in what I have to say, no matter what I write it on. I think I've made a lot of progress. I've learned a lot through CHAANGE and I'm looking forward to learning more. Do you know I went shopping on the 23rd and 24th of December with all the crowds! That was the first time I had been to a mall without my husband in 7 1/2 years and I enjoyed it and was terribly proud of myself. I also went on vacation for the first time in I don't know how long and I even took a boat ride down the river at night. It was beautiful! I have learned to let go of a lot of old attitudes,

67

old shoulds, and a lot of the panicky feelings. A couple of people have told me that they see a change in me and I see it, too, and sometimes it feels strange and it's hard to believe it's me, but I like it. I've even let go of some old relationships that were not productive and changed some attitudes toward my mother, but those two things are still difficult for me. It's also difficult to let go of worrying about what other people think, but I have done it to some extent, and will continue to work on these areas. Sometimes I feel overwhelmed by all the things that I want to change for myself and wonder if I really can do it. Sometimes I'm afraid that the changes I've made won't last, but I only feel that way about half the time, and the rest of the time I feel pretty confident. One thought that comes in and worries me when I allow it to is what I'm going to do when I'm over this and in control of my life again. I don't seem to know what I want any more, particularly concerning a job. I got married at 15 and for the most part, I've taken care of my home and my children for all these years and now my children are grown up. I no longer feel that I <u>should</u> do something that I like to do and that's good for me. Most of the time, I try to let go of this worry and just do what I need to do for me right now. I am a more positive person than I used to be. I'm more appreciative and more compassionate toward myself. I love the quote about not comparing my insides to other people's outsides. I really had been doing that. I came across another couple of lines of Walt Whitman's that I really like: "Behold, I do not give lectures or a little charity, When I give, I give myself." I feel that that's what the three of you do and I thank you very much.

and from a Holiday Inn in Florida:

Don't let the address fool you. Three hours ago I saw my <u>second</u> graduate get his diploma CUM LAUDE. My son graduated today from college and one week ago my daughter graduated from high school.

Lou, I can't begin to tell you how much I thank you and the CHAANGE program. Without the "tools" you gave me, this week would have been one of _hell,_ not excitement. I wish I could make you _completely_ understand what _18 full years_ of an albatross around my neck damn near immobilizing me - and now oh wow - today I sat in an audience in a _large gym_ - people everywhere for _2 hours,_ then 1 hour more outside in 95° weather with _PEOPLE_ - not even a sweaty palm - coming out of the gym in a crush of humanity. I'm terribly proud of my son - he's totally brilliant and going to work with a _"FORTUNE 500"_ firm for a 5-figure salary - But...he and I are both proud of _me_ - I couldn't help it - I cried like a nut! But I was _so_ happy to be a normal Mom participating in such a joyous occasion. In addition, I'd come clear here on the first trip I've been on in 8 years, eating at restaurants - some crowded, some not - staying in strange places - sleeping like a baby.

Just a week ago, I'd had my 1st "test." My daughter's graduation in a medium size gym, but no air conditioning - for a little bit I'd had a problem but my son got his handkerchief wet and I'd kept patting my face and cooled down - it got wickedly hot inside there. Your "Exchaange" letter about overheating symptoms closely correlating agoraphobia symptoms couldn't have come at a better time.

Lady, I feel freer than I have in 18 years. I feel like hugging your neck. I owe you and CHAANGE more than I can ever say.

TERRIFIC GRADUATION PRESENT

I still don't drive but I'm not worried about that - it will come. To be able to just so completely _enjoy_ these graduations - well I get teary eyed I'm so grateful. I told my son in February I'd have a terrific graduation present for him and today I delivered a proud excited (not nervous) but calm Mom here - in another state in the audience watching him graduate. From the bottom of my heart, Lou, thank you.

P.S. This letter may sound corny and darn near false - but I mean every word!!

P.P.S. I brought four of my CHAANGE sessions for support if I needed them - I DIDN'T!!!

Another major challenge we faced was exactly how to make the treatment process actually meet each individual's needs. Again, drawing on what we had observed when working with the groups, we included in the program everything we could think of which could possibly be helpful to someone who was suffering with this most severe anxiety. Our feeling was that it was all positive, constructive, healthy information - and it had the potential to be just what an individual would need to put his life back together again. Of course, all of the materials are based on our underlying understanding of the basic personality of the person who tends to develop agoraphobia, as well as our knowledge of the gaps in his development of coping skills. We realized that these are persons who are intelligent, well-motivated to get well, and that they tend to be quite intellectual in their approach. We also realized that a tremendous lack in their emotional development was actual basic information about the relationship between their bodies and their minds. We supply this information in such a way that they can take it, use it, and it can become internalized, as shown in the following examples.

From Pennsylvania:

....First, I am no longer on any medications, just vitamins. I feel as though my brain has been house-cleaned and all the cobwebs are gone. I can go outside my house with no anxiety at all now. I can have people over with very little discomfort. I can drive the car with my husband in it when we go for a ride. I can visit my in-laws and other people in the area with some discomfort. I can stay alone in the house for

long periods of time without any trouble. The only thing left is driving alone (I have only gone a few blocks so far) - and stores - that's the big one. I haven't done that one yet. I think once I get used to the other things I have done so far and can do them without discomfort, the problem I'm having with the stores should follow with, hopefully, just as much success. Or do you believe to just plunge in and do it? My relaxation is wonderful. My body does it by itself. In a very tense situation I help it along, but it still works wonders. Much better than any tranquilizer helps too. My husband and I are getting along better than ever. I feel as though I am a newlywed again. My change changed him also. I am able to help my seven year old son so much with his problems and questions thanks to your teachings on anger, resentment, etc. And I know he will be the best person possible because of these teachings. He will not grow up with guilt and anger and all the other things that are so destructive to people....

AMAZED AT PROGRESS

From a new mother in New Jersey:

....I want you to know that during my course with CHAANGE I carried a baby during the last two months of pregnancy attended Lamaze classes and gave birth completely naturally in 55 minutes. During the past two and one half months I am the sole responsibilty almost all the time for my 3 year old son and my 2-1/2 month old son (born December 1). The fatigue and tremendous energy that this present situation entails has taken away from or hampered my ability to practice my traveling and driving the way I would have liked. However, I have still made some wonderful gains and have "overcome" in some very difficult "practice opportunities."
    I am amazed at how I have been able to stay home alone day after day during a grueling winter and take care of the constant demands of an infant

and a toddler and not only have I done it, but for the most part, enjoyed it. Staying in all day used to give me panic attacks.

My ability to change negatives to positives amazes even me. You gave us those quote cards during the first weeks. Now I use Bible quotes. Every morning I wake up and repeat what Jesus said about coming to this earth: "That your joy might be full." Do you know what it does for me to open my eyes and say, "That your joy might be full?" The word _joy_ picks me right up.

Yes, I have a long way to go. I am no Ann or Faison - yet!!! But my two healthy sons and happy home are a testimony to what CHAANGE has done for me.

People tell me I look radiant or fantastic. They think it is because of my son's birth. They're right, but it is also due to the course. I really feel like I am part of a fascinating team of human beings.

I am really going on and on so I'll stop to say thank you and I'll be thinking of you in New York and watching the Today Show.

P.S.: My mom had agoraphobia and has overcome it on her own. Her panic attacks and subsequent hysteria were the big secret when I was a child. I recently let her hear Tape #1. She was stunned!!!

From the West Coast:

....Attached is my post-program evaluation which I have deliberately delayed completing to allow for the opportunity for me to practice my last big incapacity, that of travel be it being a passenger in a private auto, a bus, or a plane as well as being away from home for more than a night or two.

I am happy to report that during the last three weeks I have had many successes starting with my going to a travel agency to make arrangements for a flight from my city to a resort in southern California. Because there is no direct flight, it was necessary that I change planes each way. Just making these arrangements was a big success for me. I had no anxiety in arranging for the care of my home and dog and in packing. I do admit to some anticipatory fear in thinking about riding as a passenger in my son's car to the airport and knowing that during my two week vacation I would often be a passenger in an auto. Happily, I was very calm going to the airport. My son checked my luggage and then immediately left and I was on my own to get my boarding pass and await the passenger loading and take-off. This I did with no panicky feelings although a slight anxiety which I named excitement. I am not an experienced flyer, this being only my second trip in my 66 years and I was a little scared about changing planes in a big city, but did this with no problem and actually enjoyed the flight to the resort area.

FELT ANXIOUS ONLY ONCE

During my two week stay I did many of my inca-pacities; eating out in restaurants (originally #1 incapa-city), going to four movies (I had given this up for years), riding as a passenger in my friend's car, all kinds of shopping, meeting new people. In the entire time I felt anxious only once and that was when we started on a 50 mile trip and the thought came to me, "What if I get anxious" and, of course, I did get anxious. But I relaxed and dialogued and soon was o.k.

Before I left on this vacation, I had experienced another success, that of taking a one-day bus trip to a big gambling center. It was a big success for me to accept the invitation of friends to go on this tour. In addition to anxiety about the trip, I worried a bit about the gambling casinos, noise, lots of people, etc. After initial slight anxiety, I had a wonderful time.

I tried to mark my post-program evaluation very honestly and carefully and am amazed at how good it looks. Truly my life is better. While working on my incapacities, all sorts of other conditions in my life have improved. I am much more positive, much more relaxed and much happier. Although I am very sure about the change in me, I am not sure that others notice a change as I have never discussed my condition with anyone and have always managed to project a positive, capable, happy facade. However, at the height of the agoraphobic condition, there were times I didn't think I could go on and had it not been the responsibility I felt in caring for my ill husband, I think I would have just quietly folded. Now I can hardly believe that I felt so awful. I feel now that I am better than I ever was in so many ways. I am a very energetic person, wonderfully physically healthy, and am now able, once again, to enjoy my volunteer work, church, social and family activities. I have mentioned before that I am a new widow (nine months now) and the CHAANGE program has helped me so much in overcoming my grief. I am so pleased with my new self that I have embarked on an attempt to take off some unwanted pounds (I believe I must be the only new widow that has gained rather than lost weight) so that my outside can look as good as my inside feels.

I am now in my second week of the 15-week reinforcement program and learning and understanding more all the time. I am puzzled as to just how and why your program is so effective and sometimes I wonder if this is really true and will it last as never again do I want to go through such agonizing and intense suffering, but deep down I know that I am going to continue to get better and better. I daily give thanks to God for leading me to the CHAANGE program. It must be very rewarding to you and your associates to know that you are able to help so many people regain control of their lives.

I look forward to keeping in touch through the newsletter....

From Virginia:

It has been slightly longer than fifteen weeks since I first contacted all of you and the difference in my life and the lives of my family members is striking. Fifteen weeks ago I waited and longed for the postman to arrive with that envelope each Friday --- if he was late, it was enough to trigger a roaring panic attack. The last couple of weeks, I forgot that it was even Friday and didn't collect the mail until Saturday morning and there was not even a twinge of panic. What a relief!

SERIES OF SMALL STEPS

It has been a series of small steps until one day I could see that life had returned to normal or I should say our now version of normal. I have resumed my full teaching schedule although I have thought of Faison often in her academic setting -- even the professors have problems getting up before that entire class and presenting a course coherently. My objectives have altered somewhat -- every student is not expected to love the course or the instructor. They are only expected to complete the required material and apply the information to my course and others in the course of study. If they really like what I teach, great. If they don't, then fine. I know I have presented the material in the best way I know how and have considered each of them an individual. So be it.

Initially, as with so many of the small steps in this new approach to living, I have had to remind myself that I was doing this by choice. No one held a gun to my head, we didn't absolutely need the money to survive, this was something I wanted to do for myself. And each class has become easier, less effort, more enjoyable and satisfying. I have arranged my schedule more considerately of myself so that I have two days during the week for myself and my free-lance work. I have promised myself and kept that promise that those days are free and if I want to work, fine. If I need to rest and do what I previously considered frivolous, fine. As long as there is a choice, I can handle that well and without total exhaustion.

The pace of an active family has picked up as it always does during the fall of each year, yet this year is different. The rewarding thing--our ten year old daughter decided she needed some time to herself and stayed home from a Girl Scout activity. Our seven year old practiced talking to his body for his relaxation so he could forget his fear of his new bunk bed. We are able to discuss a possible job change for my husband without hours of what-ifs and agonizing mulling over. It is still a bit difficult to stop the looking ahead to this afternoon, tonight, tomorrow, the day after, next week, but at least I am aware of it and know where I need to concentrate my effort.

I will now start to review the tapes and materials for the next few weeks as you have suggested. All days are not totally anxiety or tension free--many times I consciously invoke the techniques and self-talking methods to get through. But with the review and constant practice, I am sure this will become less a deliberate effort and more a way of life. And this will be an on-going relationship. I know that I can always reach out if there is the time when I need help or advice or someone who just understands because they were there too.

Thank you so much for showing me I had the means within myself to turn my life around with enough effort and enough motivation.

From New York:

....I've not accomplished a great deal in the way of traveling yet, but I have had successes I'm very pleased with.

I ran upstairs to stop a cat fight, and when I'd accomplished that, the breathlessness led me into the start of a king-size panic! Without consciously thinking about it, I stood stock-still, relaxed, breathed calmly, -- and avoided the second stage of panic. My legs shook a little, but I found myself smiling and talking about the successes I'd had. Now I feel better about trying the car ride because I know I have control.

I've had thirty years of avoidance of all panic, so my progress may seem little, but I'm pleased as punch and know I'll succeed in getting control again. My attitudes are changing, and people are noticing the change.

From Indiana:

....My daughter had a baby and she had to have a C section which was unexpected, so I spent three weeks at her home taking care of her.

The great thing, before your tapes, I probably couldn't have done that. I did it (cooking, cleaning and caring for the baby) with considerable ease for me.

I'm finding crowds are also easier for me and just going, in general. If I didn't have to take this darn blood pressure medicine, I think I would be good. Ha.

I do enjoy the flyers you send out. I'm going to keep going over my tapes. That's the beauty of owning them. They're at your fingertips....

THE BIGGIE

Many times, as people go through the process of getting over agoraphobia, they are able to do all the things they had been avoiding because of their anxiety except for their "biggie." We often receive letters about this. Driving alone is often the last thing attempted, as it was for this Californian:

I'm just beginning the thirteenth week of the program, and I want to tell you about my progress.

I really resisted in the beginning - not playing the relaxation tape as often as I should. Although I could really see a difference, in that I was much less negative about things and I worried much less, I still wasn't getting out and doing things.

I got tape #12 last Saturday, and you made it

77

very clear that now is the time to start doing the "biggies." Well I heard that and I just started to cry. I could do just about anything as long as I was with someone, but I hadn't been able to go anywhere alone. Driving was the most difficult for me. I hadn't had a panic attack in quite a while, but I was sure I would if I tried to drive alone (I know that's super-negative, but I couldn't help it)!

I've kept a journal through all of this, and I started writing in it, saying, "They expect me to drive alone now, and I'm not ready, even though I've learned..." and proceeded to list all the skills I'd gotten through the program. As soon as I'd finished making the list, I realized that I really did know these things. They were a part of me, and of course I could drive alone! I got in my car right then and drove 15 miles. This was Saturday night. On Sunday, I drove further, and also started taking walks by myself (another very hard thing for me). On Tuesday afternoon, I went to the drugstore alone! That was the first time I'd been in any public place alone in ten months! The extraordinary thing about all of this is IT'S NOT SO BAD! I was excited and a little anxious, but I accepted it for what it was and didn't add any "second fear" to it. I really am in control of my life again!

Another thing I want to mention is that I saw an old friend the other day, and she wanted to know what happened - she'd never seen such a change in anyone before. She said I seemed so happy and self-confident. I knew there was a difference, but I didn't expect anyone to notice!

Thank you all so much for helping me get over this condition. I feel as if my life is just beginning!

From California, a woman writes:

My greatest concern is that my time with the program will be over soon and I only wonder if I'll be ready to be on my own. Because I'm doing this alone, I have no way of knowing if my progress has been significant. I feel, inside, that I'm a little slow but pretty steady.

I want to tell you how I've changed a pattern in my life that I thought was so deeply ingrained that change would be impossible.

On August 27, 1981, I left my job of 22-1/2 years because I simply couldn't cope with half a life anymore. The following day I sent for my cassettes.

I've been off work since 8/27/81 and will not return until the first of the year. I never thought I could be happy unless I were performing some useful service, i.e., working.

Getting well and getting in touch with who I really am is very time-consuming and my taking this time is the kindest thing I've ever done for myself. I know for certain that, without the tapes, my time alone would have been impossible.

At this stage of the program, I feel very hopeful and, at the same time, very scared. I know that very soon, I'm going to have to do those things which I've so carefully avoided for years and I don't know how I'll do.

ANOTHER BIGGIE

Restaurants and concerts are also among the last situations to be attempted by many. This letter from a woman in North Carolina demonstrates the joy one feels when they first accomplish the "biggie":

It's working!!! I made it through a dinner with 10 in a restaurant and Neil Diamond's concert. Isn't that fantastic? If you'll look back at all the problems I listed on my sheet that I had with restaurants, you'll see why I'm so proud. Little did I dream I could go to a concert.

Let me tell you how it happened. I knew I had agreed to go to dinner and the concert with one couple that we knew and three other couples we didn't know. I must have thought I was Superwoman!! Well, in yesterday morning's mail came Tape 3. As usual, I came to work with my tape player, earplugs, relaxation tape and Tape 3. You see, I have found that if I listen to the tape as much as possible while work-

ing, it helps. (I must hear it 20 times a day).

I listened to Faison and one thing she said clicked with me. She said that when she was driving and would get panicky she would repeat to herself, "I am calm and relaxed," even though she wasn't, but sooner or later, she would be. Starting at ten yesterday morning until I left work, I kept saying this to myself. Driving home to pick up my husband, I listened to Tape 3 again, then kept repeating this phrase in my mind until we got to the restaurant. What a help! When we first sat down at the table, I felt a little panic so I started repeating it again. Very quickly, I was able to relax.

I remained relaxed on the way to the concert and thought - "I've got it made!!" Wrong! Once the loud music and lights started, here came the panic *- "I've got to get out of here." I remembered that our instruction sheet for this week, #5 in fact, said, DO NOT FLEE! FLOAT WITH IT. Now, can you imagine being in a crowd of 12,500 plus, thinking, "Don't flee - float with it." Sounds funny, doesn't it? Well, can you even imagine how many muscles you can tighten and release, how many deep breaths you can take and hold, and how many times you can think, "I am relaxed," in a crowd like that? I can tell you, you would be amazed just how many and no one knows what you're doing. It's your own little secret, but it* worked! *I stayed for the entire concert and enjoyed it.*

This was such a tremendous lesson to me. It proved that you must *listen to your relaxation tapes as much as possible to begin with and you must use all the suggestions and materials that CHAANGE gives you. That's the only way it will help.*

Today I am a little jittery and tired, but I understand why. I truly put my body through tremendous stress last night. However, I'm taking this body home at two o'clock today and taking a nap. I think I'm going to like pampering myself for a change.

I just had to share this experience with someone who could appreciate my joy.

And, for many people, the "biggie" is allowing themselves to change at their own pace and with their own style of learning as is the case with this woman from Tennessee who had to deal with non-productive worrying:

....*First, I have to admit that I fought the relaxation tape. After the first time it was boring (sorry about that), and I hated having to take time to stop and listen. I found my mind wandering and I began to resent the whole plan. Then I started feeling terribly guilty to be spending so much money and not be doing what I was supposed to be - that hung around for a while. I began to worry that after exactly 15 sessions, to the minute, that I wouldn't be instantly cured, as I was sure everyone else was. I know that none of this is news to you - one of the things I have learned is that not a single one of my symptoms is unique!*
It finally dawned on me that I wasn't really on a time schedule at all - that if I kept my cassette on the coffee table with the tape ready to go, that any time I was tired enough to sit down, or a show was on TV that I didn't want to watch and everyone else did, I could put in my ear plug and "do my own thing." Some days I can't make myself do it at all - it makes me more nervous to know I have to do something against my will. I give myself permission to wait until I am in the mood. By not fighting it, I find myself enjoying them more and looking forward to the relaxing feeling. It is like taking exercise - I hate doing it, but I know that I will feel so much better if I force myself to get on that stationary bike and ride every day. I have now discovered how to do both. When I receive a new tape each week, I turn it on and ride the bike at the same time - I can do 4 miles in one session! I even ride some of the time when I am doing the relaxing tape - especially the imagery side. My bike is in front of a patio door that looks out over a mountain, and it is beautiful and relaxing all by itself. At first, I hated that side of the tape because we lived 20 years right on the ocean. The tape brought it all too close for comfort

and I would become terribly homesick. Now, we have decided to spend part of our time back down there - therefore, I am comforted by playing that side of the tape, and it conjures up pleasant memories, as well as future plans.

I think that one of the most gratifying things about this program is learning that other things in my life are connected with this phobia besides just the panic attacks. I see myself in every discussion. I shaded in every block of the agoraphobia chart! I keep asking myself, "How did they know that?" My family was terrified of me, because they never knew what would set me off in a mad explosion. They are so wonderful, my husband and 18 year old daughter - and I am sure I have abused them with words for years. But, I can't undo that - I can only try to do better in the future. I have never liked the way I look - I can't find a single feature of mine that I can point to with pride! But, since I can't change the permanent features, I can take care of myself, exercise, take my vitamins and QUIT WORRYING ABOUT EVERYTHING!

WORRY, WORRY, WORRY

I realize that I was scaring myself to death about everything. I worry about my husband dying and leaving me unable to take care of myself or fear living alone. I dread my daughter finishing college and being on her own. I read the Enquirer and scare myself to death about the demons and ghosts and flying saucers. (At least, now I know that I am doing this to myself). I finally decided to stop worrying about any of those things until I actually saw one, and then I would handle it from that point. My husband does not get home from work until 11:30 at night. I used to be too afraid to go to sleep until he drove in. Now I go to bed at 10:00, and never hear him come in. I get up much more rested after a full night's sleep. I have more energy since I realize that I wasn't overworking my body, but I was so busy fighting myself that I was almost to the point of exhaustion. Another interesting thing that may or may not be connected - I have always had a Herpes Simplex on my chin which regularly erupted during the holidays, when company was coming, etc. I haven't seen a sign of it since I started this program - and it is the first Christmas in several years that I did not have a big, oozing sore right on my chin! Stress is supposed to have something to do with them, I think.

I do realize now that I am not going to suddenly be "well," but I am learning so much about myself, and learning to like myself better. I am trying to lose 10 pounds before summer - I have an appointment to have my hair frosted in two weeks (the first time in a year that I have tried that!); I am working on my nails and skin. I feel 10 years younger already - and I hope my family agrees that I am more fun to have around the house. I still panic, I still don't drive by myself, but I can go to the store (with someone), I did go to a wedding last week - and by deep breathing - managed to be relaxed and serene. I have introduced my daughter to deep breathing, incidentally - it is helping her cope with tests and standing up in class.

I could go on and on - and I will think of things I wanted to tell you, but this will give you an idea of how I am doing at this point. I have little notes pasted all over the house that say, "I am getting better, I will get over this" - it may be helping everyone here at home....

DEVELOPING A RELATIONSHIP

Another challenge we faced was how to present the taped material in such a way that it would become an actual process of help that a person could take and use for his own growth. We knew that didactic tapes would not work. We felt strongly that the participant must actually develop a trusting, supportive relationship with the therapist which could be used as the vehicle through which the help was made possible. Our solution to this problem was to structure the presentation of the tapes in such a way that they are a dialogue between the therapist, and the two who had themselves "been through it," and then to deliver them as if they were actual therapy sessions - once weekly. In this way, we were able to include specific feelings, examples, situations, empathy, encouragement, support and, at the same time, give the participant someone with whom he can identify. This has proven to be quite effective.

From New Mexico:

I am doing very well, and I have finally been able to turn my negative thinking around to a positive one most of the time. I am able to let the negative comments of others sail over my head. I have quit trying to correct other people's attitudes and deal with just my own.

I had to laugh at the comment by Faison about the woman in the vet's office who complained about the pet store having a springer spaniel and a peek-a-poo in the same cage. They are both dogs, aren't they?

I am beginning to feel somewhat smug, like Ann, about my newfound insights into things and people. All of this has been so helpful in my job as a church secretary. Before I felt that I had to find a solution to everyone's problems. I am beginning to enjoy being human instead of trying to play God. I'm also beginning to realize that if I enjoy what I'm doing, I don't have to go out and find a higher paying job that I don't enjoy. I can please myself for a change.

All in all, I think I am coming along very well and the great thing is that I will continue to do so from now on.

LIFE NOW BUSY

From Maryland:

....I haven't written for a while so I thought I would take some time out from what has become a very busy life to let you know how I have "changed."

I think I told you in my last letter that I am now working full-time. The company I work for is a catering firm and now is our very busiest time due to spring weddings, Bar Mitzvahs and, at this moment, <u>hundreds</u> of orders for Passover food. Needless to say, since I handle the switchboard, I get all the calls. Sometimes I can't even get up from my desk for hours at a time. There is rarely a time when all six phone lines aren't ringing at the same time. Also, I have taken on some of the accounting work. It's something I have to learn as I go along because I've never done more than balance my own checkbook. There are so many people who require my services at work, in one capacity or another, that sometimes I really get tense. However, I have managed, with your help, to keep from reverting to my old habit of panicking. I know that I have to relax - and I do, even if it means leaving my desk, regardless of how busy it is, and going to the ladies room for five minute's peace and quiet and a nice little chat with myself. It's working, Lou, and I am very pleased with myself.

I am even learning to speak up for myself when things get too much for me. I can ask for what I need many times - and I usually get it. Faison and Ann were right - it is just as good when you ask.

If you remember, driving alone was my very last fear to deal with. Well, I've been working on it for the last few weeks. I now drive my car to and from work with one of my parents following in their car. I figure in another couple of weeks, I should feel confident enough to go completely alone. I know I can do it, but I need a little more time to get used to the idea - and that's okay.

I have been living with my parents for the past 8 months, but last week I took an apartment for my son and me. We will be moving as soon as school is out in June. It's very exciting, but scary, too. However, I really do want my own home so the scary will go away very soon. Just think, Lou, I will really have my own life to live - on my own, for the first time in all my 33 years! I know I can do it, Lou, and I'm really happy about that! I know I sometimes get depressed and lonely, but so does everyone else. I also know it's very hard to be a single parent. However, the apartment complex where I'm moving has a lot of single parents so there will be support. As a matter of fact, one of the girls I work with lives there and she has three children, one of whom is my son's age. She seems very pleased that we are going to be neighbors.

Another nice thing that has happened in the past few months is that I met one of the girls who participated in the CHAANGE seminar you held here in June. She is a friend of another woman I work with. It was like seeing a long, lost friend. We see each other occasionally for lunch on a Saturday or we go shopping. We keep in touch by phone, too. It's nice because we can talk about anything, especially how we feel about situations that used to scare us, and laugh about it. Many times our conversations don't even touch on agoraphobia - but it did bring us together. Quite frankly, I never thought I'd meet another Jewish woman who had agoraphobia and certainly not one who lived only 5 minutes away from me! That in itself made me feel better; I'm not "the only one."

I am so glad I took the CHAANGE course! If it hadn't been for that, I might still be in a very non-productive and harmful (to me) marriage. I don't think I would ever have had the courage and the sense of self-worth to say, "I need more", and, "I deserve more." Another benefit is that now that I am dating, I don't have to turn down a date because I'm afraid to go somewhere. In recent weeks, I have been to crowded cocktail lounges for dancing, the zoo (you have to park miles away and walk, walk, walk!), and a very crowded and noisy restaurant one-half hours drive from home. I am even planning to go to a resort city for a weekend very soon. How's that for changed behavior patterns? ....

RELAXED DRIVING

From Idaho:

After the fifth tape, I started to drive with my husband with me. Each week I was able to drive a little more, then alone. As time went by I became more relaxed with driving. I still think about driving but I know with time it will be like it used to be before my agoraphobia began.

RECOVERY

RESISTANCE

We also realized that we had to meet the phenomenon of "resistance" head on. Being acutely aware of timing, we built into the program sessions on resistance and commitment. In this way, we were able to handle that actively and positively while, at the same time, using the concept of resistance as a learning experience for the participant.

From Alabama, this participant relates her depression to resistance:

I am now in my ninth week of the program. My progress has been slow but there has been some progress.

Two months ago the idea of leaving my home petrified me. I have recently made three trips to town with great success. I have made out a schedule of times to leave home and how far to go. I try to stick to this schedule, but if I have a bad day, I stay in and rest. I try not to feel bad on the days that I don't get out. The relaxation tapes and a little positive thinking can help.

I haven't started working on my driving yet. I thought it would be easier to tackle that after I became comfortable with being away from home. I'm not sure if this is the right thing to do.

I no longer wake up in the mornings feeling nervous or depressed about having to face another day. I still have some bad days but the good ones outnumber the bad. I can honestly say that I feel better about myself and my future.

I'm still having some problems with depression. I got scared because when I started getting out and facing my fears I became very depressed. I spent a lot of time wondering why I was so depressed if I was having such success with my travel away from home. When I got my eighth tape I realized what was happening. My depression was a pattern of resistance. It was like a little bell went off in my head. I can remember when I was a child if there was anything I didn't want to do I could always get out of it by crying. My father was a real softy and couldn't stand to see me cry.

When I began to get out it scared me because it meant being around people and taking on some responsibility.

To keep from having to face these things I would cry, just like when I was a little girl and wanted to get out of doing something. When I realized why I was reacting this way it really eased me up.

It's remarkable how much I am learning from your program. It's helped me in so many ways. I still have bad days but for the first time in my life I realize that that is normal.

Keep sending those tapes!

Most people find it difficult to get beyond their initial resistance, but find, after they begin, that success builds on success. From North Carolina:

....It is incredible the successes I have been having since last week's tape about starting to actually do things that had been given up. I have had one success after another. The more successes I have, the more confidence I have to try more and more things. My life is getting better and better every day. I suppose my life is the same, but my attitude has changed so much that it seems totally different. I know that's because of everything I've learned since I started with CHAANGE but I think the real turning point was when I realized that my life is going to be better after agoraphobia than it ever would have been without it. I started viewing agoraphobia as an opportunity to grow rather than a curse.

COMPLETELY RECOVERED

From a man in California:

...I told you that some day when I felt that I was completely recovered that I would write to you. Today I am happy to report that after about two years

I feel that I am completely recovered. Since I started the program, in my initial weeks of the program I did have a few panic attacks which as time went by became further and further apart. Since the conclusion of the tape program I have not had an anxiety attack, but to be perfectly honest, there were some things that I did not do because I was apprehensive that I might have a panic attack and that would be a setback that might screw up all I had accomplished. If you would look up my records, I had agoraphobia for 27 years before I started your program. Last year I did write you that I flew to Hawaii and back with no problems although I still did not drive over bridges or go through tunnels. About six months ago, I was on a trip on a road that was strange to me and lo and behold in front of me loomed a tunnel. Since I did not have time to think about it, I drove through the tunnel with no problems. I felt very exhilarated and immediately turned the car around and drove through the tunnel again. Again the result was no panic or apprehension. I had licked the tunnel syndrome. On the trip I also encountered some bridges and did the same thing, turned the car around and drove over the bridges again. Results were the same, no anxiety or panic. Right then I realized that the only thing we have to fear is fear itself (Roosevelt said that) and if we can keep positive thoughts and attempt what we fear we probably will make it...

To top off my story, the hardest thing to face is going to a hospital to have surgery. While my surgeries were not major, removing two tumors from my face and having hand surgery for Duptyrens contracture, I still had to go to the hospital. All surgeries were done with local anesthetics so I was awake the whole time. Blood pressure before surgery was 126/82 and while they were operating in the operating room, my blood pressure was only 135/86. Please convey to all your people that if they keep trying they eventually will get better. Again I suffered for 27 years and it only took 2 years to recover.

From Tennessee:

At this point in the program, I am slowly letting go of some of those things that have caused me to get into the agoraphobic condition. It has been, and still is, a slow, hard process. I have my bad times but I am working hard at changing my bad habits and non-productive thoughts to positive and productive ones.

I know I have had a lot of resistance working against me and I know that I really have to let go of this resistance in order to do what is necessary to get over this condition.

The CHAANGE program has really caused me to look inside myself and I am amazed at some of the things I've seen - I never realized before that I'm the one that has done this to myself and I'm the one to undo it. This, in itself, has pushed me forward - I thank all of you for my progression this far.

BUILT-IN OPPORTUNITIES

We have built in, throughout the program, many opportunities for the participant to communicate with us. Most do that. Some use the telephone to communicate, but most communicate by mail. We encourage communication by mail, but do offer telephone consultations if it is felt it is therapeutically indicated. All letters are reviewed by me and either Faison, Ann, or I respond to the correspondence, depending on my clinical evaluation of the need. I then review the content of Faison's and Ann's replies to make sure that it is therapeutically sound and helpful. An example of this communication follows:

Dear Lou, Faison, Ann, et al,

....Actually, I have been putting off writing to you for some time. So this note gives me an opportunity to share some successes with you. In June my husband and I took our first real vacation in 12 years (and my first in my whole life without agora-

phobia) and went to Ireland. We flew out of Newark, N.J. and we were told to be at the airport for an 11 o'clock flight by 8 p.m. When we arrived, we found a line that wound around the terminal three times (no kidding)! We had not eaten and had to stand in line for three hours, finally getting our boarding passes at 10:57 p.m. (An agoraphobic's dream - or should I say nightmare?) I used "so what if..." over and over and was completely calm, much to the surprise and delight of my husband. Once in Ireland, there were several other misadventures, all of which I took in my stride without even mild anxiety. The highlight was a trip to the Aran Islands. A big ship crosses over from Galway, taking about 1-1/2 hours each way, but we were pressed for time so a young girl we met suggested we all take a small ferry from Doolin. The trip was supposed to take 20 minutes. The day we went, the sea was <u>very</u> rough and the fishing boat couldn't even come in to get us so we had to be rowed out to the boat in a currough (looks like a canoe and holds 5 to 6 people). On choppy seas, we had to climb out of the currough into a tiny fishing boat, capacity 12. Then the fun began. The 20 minute trip was actually an hour (the Irish call this blarney, i.e., falsi- fying time to get more passengers) with the ship tossing like a cork and the waves splashing us in the face the whole way. The girl who suggested we go was really seasick; we were all holding on, and were literally drenched. I was CALM and UNAFRAID! My husband marveled and took pictures of brave me. The whole trip was a delight, like being born again. Only an ex-ag could appreciate that feeling of joy at doing things for the first time without fear. We later learned that the waters were shark-infested and our Irish friend looked terribly upset and said we never should have gone on such a dangerous outing...

Just recently, I have had the chance to experience success in an entirely different area. I have a good friend who has terminal cancer. As one friend reminded me, it was two years ago this month that I went to visit this friend in the hospital, having panic attacks every few minutes the whole way to the hospital and *throughout the visit. Then I was surely an unlikely candidate to be of much help to him or his wife. Well, two weeks ago he experienced renal failure and was hospitalized. He frequently didn't know what he was doing and tried to pull out his catheter and I.V. The hospital was very nice and allowed friends to stay the night with him to spare the expense of a private duty nurse and to allow his wife a chance to rest. Guess who was the first volunteer for the night shift? You guessed it. I do admit to being a little nervous before I got to the hospital. I was afraid of the responsibility for knowing what to do in an emergency. But when I arrived and found out that all I had to do was to go for the nurse if my friend started pulling at his tubes, I calmed down. I spent 8 hrs. at the bedside of a dear friend who was expected to die any day and I had not one panic attack, or near panic attack. At first, I couldn't believe it myself. Of course, I was praying and I am sure that God's grace allowed me an extra measure of peace, but the skills I learned at CHAANGE were definitely called upon during this time and they worked...*

PROGRESS IN LETTING GO

Dear Lou, Faison and Ann,

Happy New Year! I'm writing to you on this yellow legal pad in my efforts to practice "letting go" of trying to be perfect, instead of writing on my engraved stationery. I call that progress----for me anyhow!

I'm sitting here at my desk and the rain is really coming down. In fact, in a nearby county (100 miles or so from here), it has been declared a disaster area and they are calling out the National Guard. I can never remember it raining so much in my 39 years. Enough of California weather update! (If the rain keeps up I'm going to have to get my canoe out - Ha! Ha!)

<u>Progress Report:</u>

I <u>can</u> now let go of: old shoulds; the need to control others; the need to be perfect. In fact today I'm nursing a horrible cold, cough and sore throat and I <u>didn't</u> put on any make-up. Now this is a real biggy for me, because I've never gone without make-up in <u>at least</u> three (3) years. I feel good being able to go today without make-up. Also today I <u>didn't</u> make my bed (cause I may need to return there) and I've never gone without making my bed upon rising. Today it's cool! - even though I have a cold.

I am accepting myself and all my anxiety symptoms and not worrying much at all about what happens to me. I don't constantly concentrate on how I feel all the time anymore. If something new happens to my body, I recognize it, accept it and go about my life, usually thinking or doing something else. I'm not that much concerned about my condition anymore (no matter what form anxiety decides to take, when it does come, it goes away as fast as it comes when I accept it and forget it and go about doing and thinking other things). It's cool!

I am thinking (dialoguing with myself) mostly positive all the time now. I do talk to myself a lot in a positive manner -- <u>whether</u> I believe it or not.

I don't drive alone <u>yet,</u> my husband goes with me, but I did go Christmas shopping. My husband sat outside either in the car or visiting with people in the mall (because he chose to) and I went into a very lot of stores alone that were really crowded with last minute Christmas shoppers all rushing every which way and pushing and shoving and I did not have any panic attacks or anxiety. I didn't even "think" about having anxiety and took my own sweet time shopping. (Before CHAANGE, I would have had to have my husband right there by my side "in case".) Thank God, I now have the freedom to shop alone. It feels good!

It's really something how the agoraphobic person has to always "be prepared" for anything and everything. I'm taking more risks now. They may seem so small to a person who takes big risks all the time, but for me, the small risks <u>are</u> big and it's my way of progressing. My small steps of progression make me feel proud of me. Since starting CHAANGE I feel 100% better about myself. It's really neat to know I <u>don't</u> have to be perfect (I was raised under the impression that I did, indeed, have to be perfect! So <u>wrong</u>, Mother!). It sure is a help in rearing my seventeen year old daughter and nineteen year old son.

Faison, thank you for replying to my letter. For now, that's my progress! Keep in touch. You are such nice folks there at CHAANGE and I really admire you for your program to help us agoraphobics....

Dear Faison,

....Even before agoraphobia, I was always pretty much a tense type person so I guess basically I always will be. Lately I began to notice that a few of the old agoraphobic feelings would manifest themselves from time to time. I found myself thinking "what if" and similar things. One day it dawned on me that I was letting old habits slip back in - so I began consciously - each time "what if" popped into my head - replacing it with "so what." I also listened to some of the tapes again, working backwards. You know, once again, the feeling of relief came over me that I had experienced before with CHAANGE.

I have a feeling I will always benefit on a conscious level from the entire CHAANGE program, just because of my nature.

I still hope you will have a program here in my area some day.

Love to all and take care...

Dear Ann, Lou and Faison:
I just wanted to drop you a line telling you that I think your program was sensational. I wrote Ann a letter last week when I suffered a most severe panic attack, but I am glad to say that I am feeling a lot better now. I think just writing things down and know-

ing that I now have someone to tell my problems and feelings to, has really been helpful. During my panic attack, I sat in bed and listened to the tapes all over again. Plus the relaxation tape was really helpful. It took me a little while, but I feel I am in control of my life again. Your program is well worth the money and time and I would recommend it to everyone who suffers with agoraphobia. I am saddened because I am now finished with the program. I know I will miss having a tape coming to me every Friday. I looked forward to that. But I will keep in touch with you. Thank you again. I am so grateful to all of you who have helped me so very much.

EASY TO OVERDO

Dear Lou, Ann and Faison,

....*I must admit that I haven't read a newsletter in months (3 or 4) - (I still have three unopened) but I read the one I just received and I loved every word of it.*

It is easy to over-do during this season and I 'specially' realized that today as I went to Penny's catalogue pick-up and felt weak and then nervous - got so shaky I had to ask for a chair to sit down and relax a moment before writing a check. That was a giant step for me to admit that to someone and ask for a chair. I have been sick and on crackers and herbal tea for three days so I'm sure that accounts for the weakness - hence the nervousness. I had triggered within me a memory of an old feeling that still is not pleasant. I was fine in a few minutes and I practiced some relaxation and positive thinking on the rest of my drive to work. I have been fine since except I'm still not strong from my virus. Yesterday I realized in the grocery store that I was, without thinking, breathing slowly and deeply to stay relaxed in there even though I was sick. So everything continues to improve and I find I incorporate CHAANGE's work more and more into my life. (My goal now is to work through all the tapes again so that I can have even more tools to apply to my life).

Come to think of it I believe it was in November of last year that I finished the program (I started in the summer but slowed down....when school started and I was once again teaching). Since then many things have happened - I went through the final hearings, etc., for my divorce which was final the first of July. In the meantime a new profession opened up for me - I am now a co-owner of a bakery. The wheels for this (after thoughts of it for 2 years) finally started moving last May, and the middle of July we opened...

Because of my job, I did a talk show on TV, a program at a Rotary luncheon, two at a spa and I don't know where all else this will lead---I'm loving every minute of it - and each time I did one of them alone, I thought, "there was a time I couldn't have done that!! - how far have I come!!" I know I did the hard work - but thank all of you for your help and support. I believe I still have many ways to change and grow but I am excited and open to that. I mainly have to talk to myself about being patient.

Happy Holidays and thanks again for your help in making my years happier!!....

CONTINUING RELATIONSHIP

As a part of the process, a monthly newsletter is sent to the participant, and a person may continue receiving the newsletter as long as he or she chooses. The newsletter allows the reader to continue to maintain a relationship as long as he feels necessary. The content of the newsletter is supportive and reinforcing of the new skills.

From Maryland:

....I wanted also to ask about receiving the newsletter. Will you keep on sending it to me. It is such a good reinforcement for what I have learned! When I read it, all the lessons pop back into my head. Some-

times, when reading it, I see myself and know then that others have the same problems I was having even if the problems were not expressly mentioned on our lesson tapes or reading material. It really does help to learn of this and sometimes the feelings of relief bring tears.

Anyway, I cannot tell you how lucky I feel that I learned of your program before things got too bad. (Sometimes I can't believe my good luck, in fact, because my learning of your program was a result of a series of coincidences)....

From Maryland again:

I started your program in March of this year and since then there has been a "change" in my life.

Prior to starting your program I was a little like Faison. I did most things but always in an uncomfortable way. Whether it was going to the stores, movies, restaurants, socials, trips, etc., the uncomfortable feeling was there. The panic attacks were there most of the time or "always around the corner." I am 52 years old and have never driven a car....

I wanted you all to know that last Monday I GOT MY DRIVERS LICENSE. This happened because of your program and you leading me on the right path to take charge of my life. I cannot say that the driving lessons, the written test and the actual drivers test were done easily and without apprehension.....but I DID THEM. I have not had a "solo" drive yet, but I know that it will be coming soon and I look forward to another success. We are now in the process of buying a car for me....

One of the articles you sent me really helped me along and it was in the exCHAANGE column (July 1981) written by Faison and Ann. "Commitment is doing it, going way past trying it, way past self-defeat, surrender and personal ineffectiveness."

I MADE IT AND I AM SO PROUD. Thank you so much.

And, from a man in Tennessee:

> I received my last tape the other day and I wish to take a moment to let you know how much benefit I have gotten from the tape program. I have had this condition for over twenty years so I have a lot of work to do in changing all the negative patterns, but I am now doing things that I have been avoiding for so many years.
>
> You certainly deserve a lot of credit for your insight and skill in developing the program and also for the warmth and human feelings which somehow come across even on the tapes. There were certainly tears in my eyes and a lump in my throat when I finished the last one. Thanks for starting me off on a new direction. I feel so much better about myself now and about life in general.
>
> I wish you and your associates the best of luck and hope the program will continue to grow and to help others. I will keep in touch through my subscription to the exCHAANGE.

HUSBANDS AND WIVES WRITE

In addition to letters from participants, we often are pleasantly surprised by wonderful letters from spouses who sometimes find the program helpful, too!

From a wife in North Carolina:

> How excited my husband and I are with our new life! So many beautiful things have happened to us since listening, so faithfully, to your tapes. It's such a blessing to have the terrible fears and anxiety he has experienced in the past, be replaced with peace and calm and such a beautiful attitude toward life. He has never wanted (or I should say felt like) to take part in things, go places or even share in the duties of a home, (that now comes so natural for him) so you might know the happiness I feel when

he joyfully cleans the house, runs to the grocery store, cuts grass, cuts down trees and saws them for the fireplace. Even cut his finger and didn't feel he had to run to the doctor. We can hardly believe these wonderful things are happening to us. And what a pleasure to go to work and not jump every time the phone rings for fear it is he wanting me to come home to give him just a little reassurance. Just yesterday he called me at lunch and said he was in a nearby town (about 60 miles away) visiting with my sister and her family. I was so thrilled. He was so excited when he came home he was like a child at Christmas. I know this seems like such minor things to most people, but I'm sure you must know the joy we are experiencing.

How grateful we are for your work and that we found you when we did. Thanks to you for CARING. It's such a special kind of love.

Another wife writes:

...As a spouse, I can say it has worked for my husband beyond belief. We prayed about the decision to ask for the CHAANGE program, we prayed for God's blessings to be on the tapes for effective results, and now the results were so effective I will continue to pray for your program and efforts to be as wonderful as they were for my husband and without a doubt, myself. A "change" doesn't come to a husband and father without an inevitable change for the marriage, family and whole household as well. Praise the good Lord for you, that's for sure.

So many young adults with todays pressure, economy, inflation and such, need this program we have found. We have told everyone we could about it and believe me if I had time to go into details about my "before and now husband" you would see why I praise the good Lord for you!...

Other letters we receive talk about spouse's reactions to the changes.

From Indiana:

This is a short note to let you know how I'm doing. I'm doing so much better now than before I started the tapes. I'm learning so much and for the first time in my life I'm really excited about growing and changing and learning that I have so many choices that I am able to make for myself and my life.

The tapes are wonderful and I'm so thankful that I decided to spend the money and invest my time in them. Thanks!

My husband listens to the tapes, too, and he is really looking at his life and using some of the life skills in his life, too.

Thanks again!

TOTALLY NEW PERSON!

and, from North Carolina:

...I am not sure exactly how to describe what it feels like to be an almost totally new person. I'll give it a try.

I have learned so much about myself that I never knew that it is even funny. I spent forty years of my life being a computer and feeling very bad if I had thoughts, wishes or actions that had not been programmed into me. For the first time ever I feel totally alive and enjoy doing what I feel is best for me. The computer blew up and I came to life.

As far as panic attacks, I have been able to do everything that used to scare me to death to think about. Most things I will have done and then the thought will occur to me that that used to scare me. That feels wonderful. Occasionally I will feel that panicky feeling for what appears to be a split second. I simply stop, identify what it is, review the situation I am in or preparing for, relax and go on about my business.

My husband says it is nice to have his wife back. He is just beginning to realize that he has a "new" wife and loves it. We have talked about this condition a great deal. We both feel that we are much closer now than ever before. He listens to almost all of my tapes and he uses the relaxation skills himself. I personally believe that this condition started for me a lot longer ago than last year. Knowing what I do now I can pinpoint things from long ago that I believe relate. All I know is that I am happy now. I feel I have more to learn to be totally in control of my life again but I am 98% there and to think I was in the hospital in December because stress controlled me.

On either tape 9 or 10 you made the statement that it is not something "out there" but within you. It makes so much sense when you think about it, but I used to try to figure out what scared me in restaurants, etc..

My boss can't believe the change in me. We have worked together for 15 years and he says he has never seen such a sparkle in my eyes. I have shared some of my experiences with him and some of what I have learned through CHAANGE. He feels that everyone could be helped by this program on some basis. Do you by any chance have a separate program that covers all the "goodies" for people who do not have agoraphobia, or is there a possible way to do one? He said he would consider making it a mandatory program for all his managers.

By the way, I thought you would enjoy knowing that at least your voice has been to Hawaii, Hartford, Richmond and various other cities. I believe it likes to fly on United best though.

This is without doubt the best money I have ever spent on anything. My husband says that CHAANGE is a priceless gift that you give yourself.

COMBINATION WORKS

We mentioned earlier that we feel it terribly important that we help people not only overcome their symptoms of anxiety and begin to do the things they have been phobically avoiding - but especially, we feel it necessary that they learn the skills which will prevent their returning again to their agoraphobic state. This involves real fundamental changes - changes in knowledge, changes in attitudes, changes in habits, and changes in behavior. We are so excited that these permanent changes can occur for people all over the world who, for one reason or another, had been unable to obtain the help they had been desperately searching for.

When she first began the program, this 31 year old midwestern housewife reported spending 17 to 18 hours each day worrying about her panicky condition:

...Just like agoraphobia is caused, for one thing, because of our combination of characteristics, so is the cure a combination of tapes, study, new thoughts and new habits. Even if I had never had agoraphobia, I would want to use this material for a new way to look at and live my life. Just think how a child would be as an adult with all of these good tools. He or she would be so well equipped for life. Thank you, all of you, for having the answer to my need. I needed more than to stop being afraid. I needed a reason to look forward to life again. I have rejoined the human race, thanks to you and to my hard work, and am enjoying it. My husband also has more admiration and respect for me than I ever thought possible. I am still working, but it is now more of a challenge than a drudge. Thank you.

This 49 year old was unable to drive alone or ride with others, and was unable to shop or go anywhere alone:

Thanks to this program I am following, my life has been busy, and I like listening to the tapes, doing the exercises, and changing my lifestyle to a much more leisure one.

105

My fears are diminishing slowly, especially the one where I was anxious whenever everyone left the house, and all I had was silence and much time to think about myself and foolish fears.

I have changed my thoughts to much more pro-ductive thoughts. I turned in to myself instead of always turning away from myself, because of the way I hated my inner feelings, and would always hurt myself by the anger I had within.

I have grabbed my thoughts by the horns and only let the well-meaning, sensible, kind ones into my mind. I refuse to let the fears, anger, hate, which I felt because of my past, into my heart and mind. When I want to go out, I go. If I want to go to the mall, I go, which is great because at one time I couldn't walk from the front door to the mail box without feeling anxious. I do travel with family or friends, not alone, but to me it's great. I know if I give myself a chance, there's no reason why I can't live a good free-thinking, wholesome-feeling life on my own, with-out help from my family.

I have learned a great deal from my past - to be humble because of my suffering; to feel compassion for those who suffer; and I want so bad to be able to get out and help others who need someone who understands, and loves people and children so much. If God is good and I do get over this, which I know I will, I would love to help people in need.

This 37 year old woman was so frightened of doctors and hospitals that she was unable to handle any kind of medically-related visit:

...I still find it hard to believe that I am an ex-agoraphobic person. Sometimes, something will come up which used to send me into panic, and my little mind will say "Uh-oh" - but, nothing happens - no panic, no terror - nothing at all. It's all automatic at this point; I just seem to switch to "calm" without really trying. Of course, there are times still when I have to consciously work at relaxing, but it doesn't

take a great amount of time to achieve "calm" anymore. The fear cycle has been broken!

It was last year this time when my condition was at its worst. I truly thought I was on my way out. I would make an appointment with the doctor, and then cancel it, make another one, and cancel that. I thought I was having a heart attack because of the tightness in my chest. I thought I had throat cancer, because I couldn't swallow. I couldn't eat; in fact I lived on cough drops and Rolaids because I felt that they helped relieve my physical symptoms. Then I would think that there was really nothing physically wrong with me at all; I was just losing my mind!

It was then that I saw the article in our local paper about CHAANGE. When I read the article, I said to myself "That's me!" That article saved my life; it felt so much better just knowing that my condition was just that, a condition, and could be treated and cured. So I signed up for the cassette program, and the rest is history.

I don't honestly know whether it was "divine intervention" or pure luck that I happened to see the article when I did; but, I hate to think in what shape I would be by now if I hadn't gone through the program when I did. With my phobia towards doctors, anything medical, blood especially, I never would've made it through these last months without the CHAANGE program.

My mother was diagnosed as having lymphoma, which is a cancer of the lymph system, and since August, we have done nothing but visit doctors and hospitals, blood tests, chemotherapy, etc., etc. If I hadn't changed my thinking and so forth with the CHAANGE program I just know that I would be a basket case by now.

I can't thank you enough for your help and support in making my life livable again. Keep up the good work.

DIFFICULTY DRIVING

This 39 year old woman had difficulty driving, going to the grocery store, and in other public places:

...I have gone from being anxious each day - wondering if this would be the day I would "fall apart" - to being quite relaxed each day. I do have some moments of tenseness - but I'm trying to utilize the "tools" from CHAANGE to help me not get into 2nd panic state. I find myself now - with much pressure off me - starting to think more long term, rather than just the survival for the day. I really do believe your program was an answer to prayer for me - as I had been praying for years for help for whatever I was experiencing. I had no idea that there was a description for it - nor that so many other "silent sufferers" were around. I am very grateful to all of you for all you are doing.

I'm still working on going to the grocery by myself - but I believe that will happen in the future. I am able to go shopping in stores now with no trouble - even unfamiliar stores. I'm so grateful.

While I was in Minnesota this summer visiting with my family - I turned on the TV and saw Lou and Faison on the talk show program - it was great.

Bless you all, and thank you for the help you have been to me.

This attorney was unable to pursue her profession because of her avoidance of places where she might be "caught" - where she could not easily escape:

I just wanted to drop you a line to tell you that not only am I over agoraphobia, but that I am better (calmer) than I have ever been in my whole life!

Last Monday I went into the hospital for <u>elective</u> surgery. About 10 years ago a lump developed on the bridge of my nose that made me very self-conscious. I knew that I should have a plastic surgeon take it off, but I was afraid to go to the hospital.

Then 5 years ago I developed agoraphobia, and the mere thought of going to a doctor caused a panic attack ----- so going to the hospital was out of the question.

Two weeks ago I <u>chose</u> to go to see a plastic surgeon, and he was able to schedule me into the hospital in one week's time. I used that intervening week to prepare myself. First I used lots of positive dialogue, and secondly imagery desensitization. While I was not totally without anxiety, it was so slight that it was almost negligible. And at the time of the operation I was <u>totally</u> free of anxiety. I was awake during the entire operation and happy ----- I know it doesn't make sense but I felt happy. Later in the recovery room I sat and talked to a nurse and was able to comfort a very nervous young girl. Me ----- of all people.

I know with certainty now that I will never again be tortured and tormented by that small voice that once told me to run. It has been laid to rest!

BEST THING THAT HAPPENED

This 34 year old man originally stated, "So far I haven't had to 'give up' any specific activity, but I maintain my existence only with the <u>greatest</u> difficulty. I have come very close to fainting in social situations (especially with close friends!) and walking (<u>not</u> riding in a car) around the block day or night can be terrifying. Riding does not seem to bother me."

Later, he wrote:

I can see it now, a brand-spanking new issue of "Reader's Digest" in every doctor's waiting room and beauty parlor with the lead article entitled, "Agoraphobia is the best thing that ever happened to me." At any rate that is certainly the case with me.

Not only do I not have panic attacks anymore, (although I do experience considerable anxiety in certain situations), I have begun to understand myself and the things that made me react to the world in the manner that I have for so long. And I'm beginning, just beginning, to be <u>at ease</u> with myself for the first time in my life. What a relief!!

And it's all due to agoraphobia and the subsequent realizations that it forced upon me; realizations that wouldn't have been possible without the CHAANGE program. Every aspect of the program so far has opened up insights, not to mention revelations, about myself that I just plain didn't know anything about before. Since a penchant for intensive analysis about <u>everything</u> is one of the non-productive habits on my list, I won't go into the specifics of what was the most important part for me, when "it" started happening and why, etc....

CAN GO ANYWHERE

When she began the program, this young woman said, "I'm still able to do things and go places that I must go, but am very frightened, dizzy, and uneasy while I'm doing them. I'm very uncomfortable alone and I find it very hard to be in a situation where I have nothing to do. I'm not able to relax and I don't enjoy things that I used to enjoy."

She later wrote:

I really want to thank you for the work you've done through CHAANGE. It has changed my life and has given me a new freedom that I never dreamed was possible.

Now I can go anywhere without worrying and fretting the whole time I'm there. That is such a great feeling to have. Over the Christmas holiday I was able to take a 750 mile trip to another state with my family and while there were some anxious moments during the vacation, I was able to see them for what they were and then to just let go of them. It was the best vacation I've ever had in my whole life. I was so relaxed that it seemed to set the mood for the rest of the family and we were really able to enjoy each other and enjoy the time together. It *was really the first time we were sorry for vacation to end.*

I really love the new me and I'm excited about the millions of more things I have to learn about life and about me. There are so many possibilities of new ways to apply all the things I've learned.

In the beginning this 27 year old had trouble relaxing, being herself, and, "accepting myself as I am."

Later on, she advised:

I have hesitated up until this point because I just didn't know where or how to begin. I have made so many changes and feel so much better about everything since I started with CHAANGE this past January. For the first time I understand what (and why) has been happening to me/in me since my agoraphobia started three years ago. And I also know what I need and want to do to get over it completely. The best part of all has been watching myself acquire the skills, internalize the skills, and see myself get better.

When I first started with CHAANGE, anything I did that took me outside of my home was a struggle, including the new job that I had just started. Now so much of that is easier that I feel great just thinking about my progress. I still have some incapacities to work on - flying, doing things independently of my husband, negative thoughts. But I'm working on them all. I know I'll be working on all of the skills for a long time after the CHAANGE tapes have stopped arriving, but I'm looking forward to it.

One of the biggest helps for me is knowing that I have a choice about everything I do. Life seems so exciting and inviting knowing that I'm not locked in by shoulds - both my own and others'. As I continue to free myself of these bonds, I feel my self-esteem and confidence grow each day and I love it. My positive dialogue with myself does wonders for my self-esteem, too.

I think that the most meaningful part of all has been in knowing that I have the ultimate control. Instead of trying to control others and situations, I can control my reaction to it. Life - as I see and experience it - can be as good or as bad as I choose. What a wonderful feeling of power and control.

I'm looking forward to receiving my last two tapes with bittersweet feelings. I've grown so much, it's sad to see it end. But yet, I know I can go back through my tapes and grow again. And that's just what I plan to do.

Thanks Lou and CHAANGE. You've been a life-saver. Because now I have my life as I choose it, not as others try to choose it for me.

THE PROCESS

As is obvious to you by now, our mission in helping people overcome agoraphobia is threefold, with each being a part of the overall purpose - to help the person become in control of his/her life again instead of having it control him/her. Our goal is to help the person learn how to deal with the actual anxiety and panicky feelings when they occur, learn how to go into frightening situations which one has been avoiding because of the anxiety, and learn the kind of coping and life skills which will help the person prevent ever having to deal with an agoraphobic condition again.

We consider this a total program; one which is not only 'treatment focused,' but, maybe even more importantly, 'prevention focused,' also.

The following letter arrived as we were putting the finishing touches on this book. We were touched by it. It was written by a twenty-nine year old man from Illinois and it epitomizes the excitement, the work, the joy, and the fundamental change which can occur for those who have been in the "living hell" of agoraphobia. His life will be different, better, and enriched because of what he has been able to do. He has truly learned the secret of life, fulfillment and happiness.

Well, where do I start to tell all of you the wonderful changes that have occurred over these past few months and to thank you for your most instrumental role in it?
I sometimes find it hard to believe the change in me; it's as if I had been holding myself hostage for all these years and have finally released myself. It's a feeling of freedom that's hard to explain (although I know you all understand it)! Life is really fun again and I know it's going to continue to get better and better as all these skills become more a part of me. I guess, for me, I was always searching for the secret to life, how to make the most of it, etc. Unfortunately in my old perfectionistic manner I created a lot of

the situations I was trying to avoid. But through your program you offered me the key to unlock those secrets. All I had to do was use that key. I must admit for a long time I did my share of resisting, figuring, "Hey, I'm smart, I understand this, now it's just a matter of time until it all goes away." Wrong! I finally realized and accepted the fact that it's not just enough to know it intellectually; I had to start applying it. After much resistance I decided, "What the heck, start doing these things you've learned," and you know (I know you know), it really works!!!

Being a graduate from college with a degree in psychology, and an analytical person to begin with, I was always searching for heavy, complex meanings, "after all, it couldn't be simple, it had to be complex." (Ha)!!

For me that is one of the most valuable parts of the program – that the answer lies within me; I am what I tell myself I am, and I feel the way I tell myself to feel. If I choose to think negative thoughts (worry, etc.) then, of course, my body reactions and feelings will be negative; and, conversely, if I think positive, I'll feel positive. Learning that the sub-conscious will work to develop any thoughts that are impressed upon it, be it good or bad, positive or negative, I continue to practice only positive thoughts. I have given up being a masochist. I might add at this point that through your program I have learned more about myself and human behavior than in four years majoring in psychology. It's so beautiful – think positive, get positive; think negative, get negative. I realize, however, that although simple in theory, as you say, it takes concerted effort and constant dialogue with myself to replace the old negative habits. With all this knowledge, my life has really changed. I look now at all my thoughts, or attitudes I have, and decide if they are productive or nonproductive. If they are nonproductive for me, I immediately replace them with positive ones. What a fantastic tool to work with! People tell me how much I've changed

- how positive I am, and you know something - I am and I love it. In fact, I really like me now. As I look back (and as you say, you really can tell how far you've come looking in retrospect) I was not one of my favorite people. I would not forgive myself for mistakes I made, I tried to be perfect, had no compassion for me, and tried to be all things to all people. Thanks to all of you and me, I'm now a new person, feeling like a new person, thinking like a new person and enjoying it all!

I could probably write a novel here about all the wonderful skills you've shown me, and how they have helped to change my life, but I will save that for my autobiography, as you suggested we write.
When I think back on all the things I have done lately that I was unable to do before, it's truly incredible. I still have one big one left on my list - to take a trip out of the state. It's been five years since I have been out of my area (although I have now expanded that area 100 fold from what it used to be). I am planning a trip out of state soon, and am looking forward to it. I know with all the skills I've learned, the trip will be nothing but a succes.

As you had discussed on the tapes, people get to the point of being glad they had agoraphobia, and I'm no exception. It's the proverbial blessing in disguise. Had I not had agoraphobia, I probably would never have had the opportunity to learn all these skills which are making, and will continue to make, my life happier, healthier, and much, much more productive!
I thank God I found your program. I hate to think what it would be like today had I not.

I really hate to close this letter. It's like saying good-bye to good friends you've just spent your days and nights with for the last 15 weeks. Although I realize it's not good-bye but a bon-voyage, certainly I am starting on a new voyage, and because of all of your kindness, compassion and understanding, it will be nothing but good!

116

As we end this book, which we sincerely hope has been of real help to you, we would like to finish with a 'wrap up' of what an individual must 'take in,' internalize, and 'use' if he successfully completes his journey with CHAANGE. The following was sent to us by Nancy H. who found it very helpful and hoped it would help others.

Nancy is married and was 37 when she began participating in the program. She was taking two kinds of mood-altering drugs, rated herself a "1" on amount of control of her life (on a scale of 1 - 10), always avoided driving, going places alone, and going to hospitals. She was very uncomfortable in grocery stores, department stores and in crowds.

When she wrote to us at the start of the program she said, *"I can go to a grocery store sometimes with my husband; and when we get there I am both afraid to go in with him or stay in the car alone! Also, sometimes when I am alone in my house and I have a 'panicky attack' I feel like 'running' from it, yet I'm afraid to run. I guess I feel I can't run from it."*

By the time Nancy sent in her evaluation at week 7, here is what she said in an accompanying letter: *"I still can't drive alone; but I have been able to drive from my mother's house to mine by myself. Of course, this is only about 1/2 block, but that is that much. I hope you don't mind my writing like this. I can express myself on paper."*

I think you will agree as you read her summation of what she learned, Nancy can express herself on paper. We are happy to share her 'gift' with you and hope it helps you have a happier and more productive life.

I have completed 14 weeks of the tape sessions. I've made a little booklet on my notes and things

I can refer to to help me. I thought I would send you a copy. Maybe it will help someone else. It seems as if it relaxed me just to _type it_! I know I am not completely cured; but I feel so much better about myself!! It feels good to know I'm _not_ crazy; and that this thing can be controlled. _That_ _in_ _itself_ is a great help! Excuse the typing errors. I don't have that great a typewriter! Keep up the great work you are doing!

My Notes from my tape sessions from CHAANGE

CHANGES:

1. Change negative thoughts to positive thoughts.
2. Change "What-ifs" to "So-whats." What-ifs shoot adrenaline. What-ifs cause fear.
3. Change patterns.
4. To grow and to change is a good thing.
5. Change your habits --- do things differently.
6. Change your systems.
7. Change your thinking attitudes.
8. Change your feelings about yourself.
9. Change anything that makes you feel better about yourself.

HABITS:

1. Break your routine habits.
   Example: Don't be so orderly. Don't worry so much about how your house looks.
2. Start developing new habits. Give up your old ones. Re-arrange the ones you don't give up, and develop new ones.
3. Don't let habits get you into a "rut." Ruts get boring.

GUILT:

1. Guilt is nothing.
2. No one can give you guilt.
3. Feeling guilty is non-productive.

4. Don't feel guilty when you really aren't. (You just feel as if you are).
5. Guilt is a habit.
6. Quit trying to "please" everybody. (That could make you feel guilty).

ANGER:

1. Don't get mad at the wrong people.
2. Don't be resentful.
3. Control your anger -- use relaxation instead of getting mad.
4. Learn just what and how much you can control. Don't try to take on the world.
5. Don't carry anger around.
6. Work anger out physically sometimes. It helps.
7. Make a list of your angers.
8. Make a statement when you are mad. It helps to get it out of your system.

HAPPINESS:

1. Be happy.
2. Happiness comes from _inside_ you.
3. Make happiness last and let it stick in your mind.
4. Remember, when you are happy, most people around you will be happy too.
5. You have the right to be happy.

DEFENSES:

1. Everybody uses defenses to protect themselves.
2. Don't worry about what other people think. They are too busy defending themselves. They are too busy thinking about themselves to think of or to watch you. Chances are, they aren't even aware of what you're doing or how you are feeling.

WHEN PEOPLE DO THINGS THAT HURT YOU, THEY ARE NOT DOING IT _TO YOU_, THEY ARE DOING IT _FOR THEMSELVES!!!_

MY RIGHTS:

1. I have the right to be happy or to be sad.
2. I have the right to privacy.
3. I have the right to be angry when I want to be.
4. I have the right to live my life the way I want to live it.
5. I have the right to express my opinion.
6. I have the right to make mistakes, and to be "human."
7. I have the right to be frank.
8. I HAVE ALL KINDS OF RIGHTS---AND THE RIGHT TO USE THEM!!!

FLOATING THROUGH A PANIC ATTACK:

1. Face it --- "I'm scared. So what?"
2. Accept it --- it's ok.
3. Don't think about the attack all the time.
4. Do things to distract yourself.
5. Take your time.
6. RELAX!!!

PANIC ATTACKS:

1. Don't anticipate an attack.
2. Anticipation is the main cause of the attack.
3. When you are having an attack, remember that people around you probably aren't even aware that anything is even wrong with you!
4. Anxiety is normal. Just remember not to anticipate that second fear. Don't be afraid of the normal part.
5. Put that second fear in a bucket and leave the bucket behind you.
6. Remember, the first fear is normal. The second fear is anxiety-bound.
7. When facing a panic attack, remember your relaxation tape and use it in your mind.
8. Don't go somewhere or do something just to prove you can. Go only when you feel like it. Don't push yourself. Go slowly.

9. What you do doesn't have to be a total success. Make yourself have small successes instead of big failures.
10. Risk doing something different.
11. Do what you can do; then pat yourself on the back for it!!
12. Your progress will be two steps forward and one step backward. Don't get discouraged!!!

HANDLING SITUATIONS:

1. Change the situation when you can.
2. Change your view; view your situation differently. The fear is _inside_ you.
3. Change your attitude from negative to positive.
4. RELAX!!

GENERAL NOTES TO REFER TO:

1. Agoraphobic people are very intelligent people!
2. Agoraphobia is a learned condition. It can be _un_-learned!!
3. Give up caffeine and watch your diet.
4. Have goals to work forward to.
5. Distract yourself when necessary -- sing, etc.
6. Listen for signals from your body. It will tell you when you are tired. Listen to it!!
7. Do one thing each day for _yourself_ -- just for fun.
8. We are all the same _deep down._
9. Repeat to yourself, "I _am_ getting better, and I _will_ get over this" every day.
10. Weird thoughts are unimportant. We all have weird thoughts.
11. Don't try so hard to compete with others.
12. Other people don't judge you as much as you think they do.
13. Don't be too quick to judge others.
14. Everything is not either black or white. There is a gray area in between. Everything doesn't have to be either good or bad (or black or white).
15. Your happiness begins with _you._

16. There is no perfect person; so don't try to be one.
17. Don't try so hard to impress others.
18. Look at your successful moments. Be proud of them, no matter how small they may be.
19. You have only so much energy. Use it wisely.
20. Don't force yourself.
21. Your condition takes energy. Conserve it and use it wisely.
22. Do things for you.
23. You will have normal anxiety. Just watch that second fear!
24. Your successes are important - no matter how small they are.
25. Don't worry about the world. You have enough "monkeys" on your back. Don't take on any more.
26. Exercise your rights.
27. Don't try to please everyone. Please yourself.
28. Don't feel that you need approval.
29. You have the right to be you.
30. We all have limits. Don't go over and beyond yours.
31. Take time for yourself.
32. Love yourself for what you are.
33. Feel good about yourself.
34. Be able to take rejection.
35. Do one thing at a time. Go slowly in what you do.
36. Stop beating yourself up.
37. Don't close your brain to what you think you don't understand.
38. Get rid of fear inside yourself.
39. Fear is inside you.
40. Talk to yourself.
41. Let other people do things for you.
42. Don't try to be perfect.
43. Be human.
44. Think positively - not negatively.
45. Don't feel obligated to anyone.
46. Remember, you will have good days and bad days. Don't get discouraged!!

BEGINNING AGAIN:

1. Do the things you are afraid of. (Remember NO SECOND FEAR!!)
2. Observe and notice.
3. Understand.
4. Experience.
5. Will yourself to get over this situation.
6. Practice what you've learned.
7. Accept the anxiety. Remember, anxiety is normal.
8. Don't let that second fear overcome you.
9. Feelings are memories.
10. View anxiety as excitement.
11. Remember, anxiety is normal, but second fear is controllable.
12. RELAX!!!!!
13. Practice being unafraid everyday!!

AFTERWORD

"I felt so alone."

"My family never understood."

"I never knew anybody else who had what I had."

"I thought I was the only person in the world who suffered this way."

"This has been my private hell."

These are the statements we hear over and over again. I would guess that almost every person with whom we have worked, no matter where they live, no matter their age, no matter how close-knit their family or how alone they are, has felt much the same way. It is sad that this feeling of aloneness and separateness is also a burden of the person with agoraphobia, because just the opposite is true. There are many who suffer.

We chose to end with Nancy's personal notebook so that you can feel a connection with another who has had agoraphobia, and also to give specific suggestions from one who has <u>overcome</u> it. As you know by now, overcoming agoraphobia is a process of learning new skills, behaviors, thought patterns and attitudes that are productive and not fear-enhancing. For most people this requires some sort of a structured process, such as the one we offer. For others, it is possible to stop frightening oneself by consistently <u>refusing</u> to allow it and by relaxing, both in body and in attitude. We believe that the tips you have heard from the dozens of people who have contributed to this book can help those of you who are suffering as they did. We sincerely hope so.

You have heard people talk about the importance of understanding what is happening when one has agora-phobia, that it is the body's reaction to an overload of stress and anxiety, that the panic is an adrenaline reaction - the body's fight or flight reaction - and that it is a normal physiological response to fear of any kind. Those with agoraphobia are not crazy and will not go crazy from it.

You have heard from people the importance of relaxing and of continuing to relax and rest, even when it may feel as if it is not helping. You have learned that one needs to do this so that the relaxation response will become internalized as a skill that one can draw on and use to combat stressful and anxious feelings throughout life.

You have learned that those with agoraphobia are sensitive persons - sensitive to lights, to sounds, to medication, to food additives, to feelings - tending to "take in" things from the environment more than do people who were not born with this sensitivity, and you have also seen, through letters, that many have come to value this sensitivity and to make allowances for it, mainly by not expecting that they "shouldn't" feel this way!

You have learned that most people with agoraphobia are intelligent, and are typically dependable and competent, with an exaggerated need to be in control. They are sensitive to criticism, and do not understand the connections between the mind and body, not allowing for adequate rest or normal relaxation.

You have heard from many who described how, at a time of stress, their body began reacting with panic attacks, with anxious feelings, with feelings of dread or impending doom, and, sometimes, with strange, seemingly uncontrollable thoughts. You have heard how they began monitoring their body symptoms and worrying about the feelings - when they would happen again, why they were happening, what that meant, who would see them, whether or not it would kill them or cause a stroke or heart attack.

You have read many letters written by people as they went through the process of overcoming those fears, of coming out of the spiral of anxiety. Much has been said about patterns and habits, and the need to practice, practice, practice the new patterns so that they will become automatic, just as the fearful ones were. Much has been said about understanding and recognizing and dealing productively with angry feelings.

Several people have talked about resistance to change, resistance to doing things that are new, and, therefore, uncomfortable. You have read letters from others who talked about how their relationships and on-going family systems changed when they began to change. You have read of people who came to terms with the fact that they have individual rights and the right to claim them!

We hope, too, that you have learned about purpose from those who share with you in this book. Personal purpose, to us, is such an all-encompassing concept and is crucial in overcoming agoraphobia. We think that coming to terms with your own purpose in life can release you from all the "shoulds" that have been hampering you, can help you become assertive, can help you in letting go, and can make the difference in having a productive life of your choosing, instead of living according to the proscriptions and wishes of others. We have seen people who have truly internalized the meaning of purpose and have changed their lives almost overnight.

These are the ideas, thoughts, insights, and challenges that we hope you have received from this book. This was our intention. We know how hard it is for those who suffer with this devastating condition. We would be pleased to hear from any of you who wish further information about our programs. We do have available a free packet and tape, which can be obtained by writing:

CHAANGE
1339 S. Wendover Road
Charlotte, NC   28211

Good luck to you.

GLOSSARY

Of terms as used in this book

Adrenaline -   The flow of this hormone into the
                   blood stream is what causes bodily
                   symptoms such as hyperventilation,
                   increased heart rate, dizziness, sweat-
                   ing, hot and cold flashes, numbness,
                   weakness, trembling, and many others.
                   Adrenaline can be emitted when
                   a person is frightened, either by
                   something real or by what he anti-
                   cipates may happen.

Agoraphobia -   The Diagnostic and Statistical Manual
                   of the American Psychiatric As-
                   sociation defines agoraphobia as
                   the "marked fear of being alone
                   or being in public places from which
                   escape might be difficult or help
                   not available in case of sudden in-
                   capacitation."

Anger -   References to anger and to angry
                   feelings are found in this book because
                   it is an emotion which many of
                   us have never learned to deal with
                   productively. In the tape program
                   we devote one entire session to
                   this subject. We find that people
                   with the agoraphobic personality
                   tend to misunderstand anger, try
                   to not show anger, and also tend
                   to misinterpret the body reactions
                   related to anger.

Anticipatory Anxiety - Every person with agoraphobia
knows that feeling of dread a few
hours (or days) before doing something
that has caused a lot of panicky
feelings in the past. This feeling
often sets a person up for the very
symptoms that they so fear. It
is for this reason that much effort
is spent helping people learn to stop
that habit.

Assertiveness - Because assertiveness involves taking
control of one's own life and being
responsible for oneself, we stress
the individual person's rights, while
stressing one's responsibility to others.
Assertiveness is an attitude or philosophy in which one assumes re-
sponsibilities for his own happiness.

Avoidance Behaviors - Most people who suffer with
agoraphobia find themselves avoiding
certain situations or events, making
excuses, or perhaps being unable
to stay home alone. Most frequently
avoided are driving, going to church
or synagogue, going to shopping
malls, going to grocery stores, sitting
at the barbershop or beauty parlor,
driving out of town, driving over
bridges, through tunnels, or flying.

Biggie - The biggie is often the last avoidance
situation an individual tackles. This
term seems to have come into being
spontaneously over the years and
refers to the avoided situation that
causes the most panic for the individual and seems to be the hardest
to overcome. In many it is the
thing that is done infrequently such

as flying, driving out of town, attending weddings, going to the doctor or dentist, staying alone overnight, etc., because there is not as much opportunity to practice as there is for some of the more common situations. The biggie can be accomplished with repeated practice and with positive self-statements.

Caffeine - Caffeine is a stimulant and the person with agoraphobia is already stimulated enough. We suggest that everyone who suffers with the condition of agoraphobia immediately give up all caffeine, including coffee, tea, chocolate and all cola drinks, or any soft drinks with caffeine in them.

Depression - Because agoraphobia is such a devastating condition, in which a person feels a certain sadness and loss for the person he used to be, depression is often a part of the agoraphobic condition.

Development of Agoraphobia Chart - This chart helps a person delineate his own background and personality characteristics which have contributed to his development of agoraphobia. This includes such traits as sensitivity to stimuli (such as lights, sounds, medication), separation anxiety, many rules, naivete about body and feelings, alcoholism in the family, many "shoulds," a need to be in control, competence, capability, dependability, extremely high expectations of oneself, and a sensitivity to criticism. The chart then goes on to graphically illustrate how such a person, at a time of stress, begins to fear his body reaction rather than understand it, and thus, gets involved in the spiral of agoraphobia.

Dialogue -   Most people with agoraphobia find themselves in a constant dialogue with themselves and others about this condition. This dialogue is usually negative and nonproductive, filled with such statements as, "what if" and "I can't." Working on changing one's dialogue is an invaluable part of overcoming agoraphobia.

Distraction -   During a time of panic or of worry or of anticipatory anxiety, one of the techniques that we advocate is distraction. Anything which changes the focus of a person's fear-enhancing thoughts can be helpful.

Habits (patterns) - By the time a person has developed agoraphobia, his behavior encompasses patterns or habits which contribute to his fear. Understanding that is the first step to getting in control of it and helps one realize how much work and repetition is really required to unlearn (break the habit) this condition. Not only are the learned behaviors ingrained as habitual, but so are the self-statements related to the condition.

Imagery -   The CHAANGE relaxation tape has progressive muscle relaxation on one side and relaxation through imagery on the reverse side. Relaxation through imagery involves going through a process of "putting oneself in a relaxing spot" (such as at the beach) and thinking about all the pleasant feelings and sensations involved in that.

Panic Attack (anxiety attack, terror attack) - These words are interchangable and describe feelings which seem to come out of the blue for most people. They are characterized by the urge to run and the feeling that one may die, have a heart attack or a stroke or may lose control, go crazy, or painfully embarrass himself. Many people have palpitations, dizziness, weakness, difficulty breathing or swallowing, sweating, numbness or upset stomach. Others may fear that they will vomit or lose control of their bladder or bowels during the attacks.

Positive Suggestions (affirmations) - As a way of helping the person change his negative, nonproductive, fear-enhancing dialogue, positive and productive sayings are included in the program. These positive suggestions are called affirmations by some people. They are amazingly effective and helpful, even though they often seem simple.

Practice Opportunities - A setback is not a setback unless one calls it that. We find it more helpful to call any anxious feelings or difficult situations practice opportunities since that is what they really are - an opportunity to practice your new skills of thought, dialogue, and behavior and a chance to replace the old patterned response with a new and productive one.

Process -   In this book we have used the word process in many different ways. A process involves knowledge, skills, and practice utilized over a period of time, rather than intellectual knowledge alone.

Relaxation -   In addition to relaxation through imagery, we teach progressive muscle relaxation. This involves learning to systematically tense and relax muscle groups. We suggest that people in our program practice this relaxation ten times per day!

Resistance -   Resistance is a universal phenomenon. Everyone resists change in his or her own way. It is important for one to be aware of his own patterns of resistance so that it does not interfere with his progress.

Setbacks -   A setback is described by people with agoraphobia as a time when they revert back to old patterns of panic. We prefer the more productive term, practice opportunity.

Shoulds (or shoulds list) - Shoulds are all of the things a person feels he or she ought to do in order to be a "good" person. Sometimes people are shocked by the sheer length of their "should" lists! Some have noticed immediately that most of the "shoulds" on that list are not theirs at all, but are carry-overs from years ago.

Slush fund -   A phrase describing old angers which have not been resolved.

Stress -   Any event requiring a homeostatic response. Some of the stresses which often precipitate agoraphobia are a move to another city, having a baby, illness, relationship problems, a job promotion, death, surgery, a new home and many others.

System -   A system is a combination of parts forming a complex whole. When we talk about making changes and its affecting others, we are talking about changes in a system. When one person changes the others around him or her are bound to be affected in one way or another.

Weird thoughts - Many people who have agoraphobia have recurring disturbing thoughts which are difficult to shake and which they often refer to as weird thoughts. It is so important to re-member that everyone has weird thoughts, but not everyone frightens himself with them. Letting go of worrying about them and of frigh-tening oneself with them is the way to overcome them.